CISTERCIAN FATHERS SERIES : NUMBER FORTY-FOUR

JOHN OF FORD

SERMONS ON THE SONG OF SONGS, IV

JOHN of FORD

Volume Four
(SERMONS 47–61)

Translated by
WENDY MARY BECKETT

CISTERCIAN FATHERS SERIES : NUMBER FORTY-FOUR

SERMONS ON THE FINAL VERSES OF THE SONG OF SONGS

CISTERCIAN PUBLICATIONS: *Kalamazoo, Michigan 1983*

The editors wish to express their appreciation to Mr John Nixon for his help in preparing the manuscript for publication

This translation is based on the critical Latin edition of the sermons prepared by Edmund Mikkers and Hilary Costello and published in the series CORPUS CHRISTIANORUM, *Continuatio Mediaevalis* XVII & XVIII.

Latin title: *Ioannis de Forda, Super extremam partem cantici canticorum sermones cxx.*

Available in Great Britain and Europe through

A. R. Mowbray & Co. Ltd St Thomas House
Becket Street, Oxford OX1 1SJ

Library of Congress Cataloguing in Publication Data (Revised)

John, Abbot of Ford.
Sermons on the final verses of the Song of Songs.

(Cistercian Fathers series ; no. 29, 39, 43, 44)
Translation of Ioannis de Forda Super extremam partem Cantici canticorum sermones CXX.
On Spine: on the Song of Songs.
Includes bibliographical references.
CONTENTS: 1. Sermons 1-14—2. Sermons 15-28.—3. Sermons 29-46.—4. Sermons 47-61.
1. Bible. O.T. Song of Solomon—Sermons. 2. Catholic Church—Sermons. 3. Sermons, English—Translations from Latin. 4. Sermons, Latin—Translations into English. I. Title. II. Title: On the Song of Songs.
BS1485.J6413 223'.907 77-3697
ISBN 0-87907-629-1 (v. 1) AACR1
ISBN 0-87907-644-5 (v. 4)

Book design by Gale Akins.
Printed in the United States of America.

TABLE OF CONTENTS

SERMONS

SERMON FORTY-SEVEN

The beginning of the forty-seventh sermon. What is meant by the bride's beauty, her sweetness, her comeliness, the terror she arouses.

'YOU ARE BEAUTIFUL, MY LOVE, sweet and comely as Jerusalem, terrible as an army encamped in battle
Sg 6:3 array.'*

The spouse lavishes his graces on his bride, inciting her to give him thanks for them. It may be gratitude because he himself has sought for one who was not first seeking for him, or it may be because, when he has found her, he lets her search for him in return. Or it may be gratitude for the way in which, after she has sought him, he presents himself to be found, or the way in which having been found, he never appears empty handed. For he heaps new blessings on the old, and surpasses what he gave at first with what he still has to give. Is there one of these graces that is not an extraordinary favor, something quite special, a most powerful means of rewarding her? Does not each of them claim her whole heart in payment? At first, she was sought without her knowledge and perhaps, even without her assent, but from that state of ignorance and unwillingness, she became knowing and willing. So, after a long search, she was found, and then, in case she lost herself all over again, from being found she was taught to seek him who had sought and found her. But the search might be too much for her, she might not have the staying power, and so, as she sought, the one whom she was seeking came to meet her. Now at last he is found, yet there must be no danger of his seeming to be found in vain, and this is why he comes to meet her 'full of grace and truth!'* *Jn 1:14*

Wherever the bride turns, there is grace. Even before she began, at the very first steps that led to her finding him, on the paths by which she drew nearer to him, at the joyous brevity of her paths, at the recompense that she awaits as her reward: at each turn, there grace has been, grace anticipating her, leading her to itself and, at the very last, grace crowning her. Yes, grace has made a covenant with her chosen ones,* she has sworn it by her holiness, she has struck with them a lasting treaty and she will never take it back.* Blessed indeed is this generation, sought like this and seeking like this!* And among this generation, the happiest of all is the one who has surrendered her soul to the grace that has gone before her, to be for ever a whole burnt offering. She is never satisfied with what she has given, for she can never be unaware that it is not enough.

Cf. Ps 89:3

Cf. Ps 89:34

Cf. Ps 24:6

2. Every soul like this will be rightly thought worthy of having the name of 'bride' or 'loved one'. Among the number who are seeking and the throng who are running, she seeks with greater earnestness, she runs with greater speed. She traces the Lord more

skillfully, she follows after him more tirelessly, she finds him more joyously, she holds him more tenaciously. But you may ask, what is the outcome of all this great labor? What reward is there for these investigations? If you find what you are after, what is the result? The answer is: the spouse's blessing, and that blessing many times over, in proportion to the hard work that went before! So Jacob, after some wrestling with the angel, wrested from him a blessing that was far from slight, and in consequence, changed from Jacob into Israel. In other words, the painful struggle of wrestling and refusing to admit defeat, brought him a share in the vision of
Cf. Gen 32:24 God.*

Now, this blessing was not just for the time being, as if to wish him well on his journey! No, the angel's words were: 'Your name
Gen 32:28 will be Israel.'* That is to say, he was not a man who had seen God or who would one day see him, but a man who was actually seeing God now, always living in the presence of the
Cf. Ps 16:9 God he saw before him,* a man who could say with Elijah, 'The Lord lives, and I stand
1 Kgs 17:1 before him.'* So great was the grace of the blessing that henceforth filled Jacob—or rather, not Jacob now, but Israel—that afterwards, in the land of Canaan, he went
Cf. Gen 32:31 limping.* But, from that day on, Israel set his foot firmly on his true inheritance, for now he was wise about 'the things that are above, not
Col 3:2 those that are on earth.'* So, as he said himself, he saw 'God face to face, and his life was
Gen 32:30 preserved.'* The face that saw God exteriorly, gave a wonderful light to the interior face, so

that he could see God interiorly, and he made great strides towards longing and hoping to contemplate the Light of God eternally. All this gave him an unshakeable pledge of salvation, so that he glories in having been saved. As a man filled with God, he put his trust in the Holy Spirit, and he heard his answer in all that happened, assuring him of the certainty of salvation.

In this wrestling, the bride is certainly no weaker than Jacob, but, on the contrary, much stronger, having had more experience in it. Not only that, but she shows much greater power in having to wrestle, not with some angel, but with the Lord of hosts himself, whose name is 'the All-powerful'.* This *Cf. Ex 15:3* is a glorious combat, and her hope is that it will end in extraordinary and memorable blessings, for she has fixed and settled determination not to let God go, until he has blessed her.* God is a more powerful wrestler *Cf. Gen 32:26* than the angel, but then, he is also a more lavish giver of blessings.

3. In fact, every word the spouse says to his bride is a blessing: 'You are beautiful, my love, sweet and comely as Jerusalem, terrible as an army encamped in battle array.'* Every *Sg 6:3* single word of this pours out the dew of blessing, so that everything that they contain within them blooms and becomes exceedingly fruitful, because of the exceedingly heavy dew. The bride's beauty has been commended by the spouse in previous words, indeed, it is this very commendation of her beauty that seems to have aroused, not merely the companions of the spouse, but his

own heart, too. He is aroused to a wondering eulogy, repeating her commendations again and again, as he does here.

Firstly, we heard: 'Behold, you are beauti-
Sg 1:14 ful, my love, behold, you are beautiful!'*
Secondly: How beautiful you are, my love,
Sg 4:1 how beautiful!'* Thirdly: 'You are all beauti-
Sg 4:7 ful, my love, and there is no flaw in you.'*
The first time the praise is repeated, there is a note of wonder, and attention is called to it. The second time, although it is the same expression, the note of wonder has grown into a sort of intense amazement. The third time, there is the same repetition, but raised to the highest pitch of eulogy, for she is described as 'all beautiful', and this is further amplified by saying 'she is without flaw'.

4. What more can possibly be added to commendations so many and so ample? What does it mean that then rich praises should be followed by words much plainer and much more restrained, that he should say simply
Sg 1:14 and plainly: 'You are beautiful, my love'?*
The reason is perhaps that the bride after hearing her beauty so often and so highly extolled may learn to recognize its true measure, and to realize that if she is still in need of blessing, she cannot yet be perfect. For the spouse blesses when he praises, and to be blessed by him means to have received some fresh gift of grace from his mouth.

So the spouse bestows his blessing on his beloved, calling her beautiful, confirming her still more in the beauty in which she is now pre-eminent, while at the same time decking her with the regalia of a new beauty. For, as the apostle says, 'our inner nature is renewed from day to day,'* while it proceeds from brightness to brightness in the perception of our true image, which is Christ.* In my opinion, the bride's beauty is described in this particular place because she has reached the point of being allowed, in her turn, to contemplate the very beautiful face of her spouse and to carry away from that contemplation very great brightness. Therefore, the praise that is offered her is more modest than usual, as was pointed out above, since the increase in her beauty brings with it an increase in humility, the one inviolable safeguard for anything beautiful.*

Cf. 2 Cor 4:16

Cf. 2 Cor 3:18

Cf. Bernard, SC *45.2; SBOp 2:50; CF 7:233.*

5. Likewise, she is called 'beloved', because she who now has the privilege of loving, was first of all loved herself, or if not because of this then certainly, because she has been allowed to share in the secret thoughts of God the Father. This is the true definition of divine friendship, having its foundation in what is above and not in the things we men know. Listen to what is the entire basis of this friendship: 'I have called you friends,' says the Lord, 'because everything I have heard from my Father, I have made known to you.'* He says, 'I have called you friends', that is, 'I have made you into friends.' This is how I have done it: I have revealed to you the secrets of my Father's love, I have manifested the glory of God, I have unveiled to you the joys of heaven and led you to them through hope and desire, having first weaned you away from earthly desires.'

Jn 15:15

The bride has a right, then, to be called

'beautiful', because she has despised all things of earth to concentrate wholly on the Beautiful One. And she has a right to be described as 'my love', because she loves him who alone is lovable, because there is not one of the mysteries of heaven which she has not been told by her spouse and her love, because he reveals more and more, her progress through the degrees of love keeping pace with her growth in understanding, Moreover, now that she has been taken into partnership by the Word of God, it could happen that the grace of such great beauty and friendship made her too majestic in the eyes of her associates, who have perhaps not progressed as far, or made her less accessible to them, or less kindly of manner. So her gifts of grace receive one grace more, to ensure that the more graciously pleasing her spouse finds her, the more graciously pleasing she is to those who share her partnership of grace.

6. But notice carefully that while calling her sweet, he adds the word, 'comely'; thus she may be pleasant though eschewing levity, cheerful yet excluding frivolity, mild without trace of fickleness, approachable without being common, affable yet not forward, not grudging of speech nor yet prodigal, sweet so as to warm everyone with pleasing cheerfulness, yet upright so as to instruct others by the example of her gravity. In her sweetness, she is eager to anoint everybody as if from the abundance of her own anointing; in her comeliness, she sets to work as if to shape everybody into the likeness of her own overflowing loveliness. In short, she sets herself

to please everybody so as to bring them to grace, and she tries eagerly to become everything to everybody, so as to bring them to salvation.* *Cf. 1 Cor 9:22*

7. This is why it is expressly said, 'Sweet and comely as Jerusalem',* for this friend of God has learned to make herself resemble that entire city of saintly inhabitants. She is lovable to all, useful to each one individually, and an object of respect for all of them together. And look at the arrangement of phrases in this eulogy. The first thing the spouse says of her is that she is 'beautiful', but he does not say, 'beautiful as Jerusalem'! He plainly refers to that beauty by which after gazing with her inner eye of contemplation she has tried to conform to the eternal beauty of the spouse. Therefore his praise takes as its starting point that which is the origin of all that is found praiseworthy. Quite clearly, 'all the glory of the king's daughter is from within.'* *Sg 6:3* *Ps 45:14*

Besides, although she receives an indestructible loveliness from her close union with the Word, an increase of sweetness and comeliness comes to her from her association with her fellow citizens, too. In her charming and holy intercourse with them, she bestows grace on all, and yet she herself grows in grace from each single encounter. This is why she is 'sweet and comely as Jerusalem'*: she makes Jerusalem sweet and comely, and she in turn is made sweet and comely by Jerusalem. It is not a question of the beauty of her beloved claiming her so solely and totally for itself alone that she loses all eagerness for the *Sg 6:3* sweet and comely things that are in the beauty of the daughters of Jerusalem as well. No, she knows that the loveliness of her spouse has many forms, and it has illuminated with its comeliness the face of every single one of them. Consequently, she has learned, in each one of them, to see with wonder her spouse, unchanged, and to do him reverence. All this has now brought her to a beauty that has many forms, for in every face, her beloved shines out at her, her beautiful one shows himself to her. She is crowned with an overwhelming glory of comeliness, longing as she does, not only to give pleasure to everyone, but to be pleasing in what she has received from them.

8. Yet she arouses intense fear, for her admiring description continues: 'Terrible as
Ibid. an army encamped in battle array.'* Are we to conclude that the bride is about to set out for the battlefield, seeing that she has provided herself with the gear of war and so carefully made herself ready for it? Did not her beloved proclaim to her a ceremonial sab-
Cf. Is 58:13 bath?* Is not her life hidden in the shelter of
Cf. Ps 31:22 his presence?* Is not she the very one who so short a time ago was glorying in the words, 'I am my beloved's, and my beloved is mine,
Sg 6:2 he pastures among the lilies'?* Is this the song the bride now hears: the terrible flare of the trumpet announcing that the quiet days of love are over and a new war lies before her?

But the bride herself knows only too well, knows and cannot but know, forced as she is to experience it without intermission, that her spouse has enemies. His enemies are of great strength, too, ready to do anything that will dissolve the sacred marriage bond that binds her to a spouse such as he. They are envious of a union so blessed, tortured to see them kissing, furious at their embracing. To hear them praising each other makes their enemies pine away with anguish; when the lovers rejoice, their enemies lament, and their gladness fills them with rage. These are the enemies of charity, and when they see it blazing up, they burst into flame with it. In fact, the flames of love burn them very much more than the flames that are natural to them.

Inflamed as they are by these 'coals, red-hot, blazing',* and experiencing time and again the violence of these fires, they realize they will never be able to reach the mysteries of the king's bedchamber. They despair completely of ever being able to come anywhere near them. And yet, they are still unable to call a halt to treacheries and ambushes or admit the hopelessness of their evil designs. They have set their heart on harassing someone whom they cannot disturb at all, and although they have no courage, they do have great powers of exertion, of attack and persecution.

Cf. Ps 120:3

But what can be the outcome of these labors spurred on by envy? The bride has the strong support of her beloved, and he is there to protect her love just as he was there to bestow it on her, and will be there to reward it. When she said, a little while before, 'My beloved is mine',* what did she mean except that her beloved is everything to her? 'If an army should rise against me',* my beloved

Sg 6:2

Ps 27:3

is my shield and sword, my breastplate and helmet, in short, all the armory of war. My only occupation is to keep myself for my beloved and cleave to him. All the fighting will be done for me; my beloved will see to it, and I have only to be still. Let my enemies array against me as many stratagems as they please, let them hatch their plots and draw up their lines of battle: my beloved is with me, 'though a thousand fall at my side, and
Ps 91:7 ten thousand at my right hand.'*

9. In this way, the spouse has established the bride on a pinnacle of confident hope. In all the attacks of the enemy, hope has taught her to take comfort in her beloved himself, and not only to remain fearless in her heart, but even to appear terrible to the enemy as well, because of her repeated triumphs. But if it is to the daughters of Jerusalem we want to apply this phrase, then it will be seen to refer to them also. Not infrequently, the face that the bride shows them seems to them 'terrible', so that she appears cruel, when she is no more than grave. She is acting as the wise man advises: 'You have daughters; guard their bodies, and do not let them see an indulgent
Sir 7:26 countenance.'* For what else is symbolized by daughters, the weaker sex, except the feebleness of weak souls? They are sadly scatterbrained, and it is a great help for them to be met with a dignified expression. Their immoderate craving for frivolity is checked by a certain fear that comes from a suitable gravity. It is as it were repressed by the bridle of discipline. Hence we find holy Job saying:
Job 29:8 'The young men saw me and withdrew.'*

'I smiled on them when they had no confidence, and the light of my face was not cast away.'* *Job 29:24*

So then, after the spouse has praised the remarkable beauty of his bride, which comes from her continued gaze on him, and after he has also praised the sweetness and comeliness with which she strives to please and benefit everybody, he comes at last to commend her seriousness. (It goes of course, without saying, that this seriousness is the effect of love, and not of severity.) Yet if we only regard the outer appearance, there is nothing to choose between the passion of ardent zeal and that of bitter cruelty. The bride has certainly put away her mother's face and assumed that of a prosecutor, pitiless, remorseless, fierce and impassioned.

But even the frenzy of prosecutors restrained its rage within the fixed bounds of legality, so as to follow the judicial procedure laid down by their predecessors. By these means the verdict, issuing as it did from a tribunal and being considered, not precipitate, seemed all the more terrible. It is just the same when the bride sets herself to act sternly. It is a judicial severity she aims at, deliberately putting on an official cloak of zeal with a punitive intention. She conducts a searching cross-examination, she makes her points rigorously, and apparently forgetful of her maternal breasts, she seems to be abandoning the children of her womb. At that moment, then, the impression she gives is rather of severity than of sweetness and comeliness 'like Jerusalem';* she is more like a line of *Sg 6:3* battle ready for the fray, because she feels there must be no derogation from the fair demands of justice. She feels an implacable anger against her own flesh and blood, considering that to spare them would stamp her as guilty of an offense.

10. But he who knows the inmost secret of his bride's heart and mind,* calls her 'terrible', not cruel. What he is especially commending in her is the way her degree of love regulates the measure of her zealous enthusiasm. It is truly love that sets this enthusiasm on fire, just as prudence gives it a keen edge and a sense of justice balances it and fortitude makes it bold and temperance controls and tempers it. In as much as her moderate conduct allays the terror of this zeal. What begins in love cannot but end there.

Cf. Ps 7:10

Besides, the 'camp of God' is an army of the virtues I have just named, a camp exceedingly strong, and, as scripture says, 'uttering his word.'* Around the bride, these virtues are encamped like a great rampart, and they do indeed make her terrible to her enemies, at every point. And she is not terrible to her enemies alone, but also, as we have seen, to the maidens, who are still in need of the rod of correction. In her role of 'an army encamped in battle array', the bride wages war on her maidens, shoots her arrows, deals out wounds, pursues their utter ruin. Amid all this, though she may seem to the daughters of Jerusalem to have been sundered from her motherly affection, she reposes quite tranquilly because of what she hears her spouse saying within her. Whatever the insults of her

Joel 2:11

daughters, he has only praise, as if he were telling her: The reproaches of the maidens are not to upset you; only have charity, and do what you choose.* It is good for them to think you terrible, they are not yet worthy of seeing how lovable you are. 'If you have loved them in the wrong sense, you have been their enemy. But if you have been their enemy, in the right sense, then you have loved them!'*

**Cf. Augustine,* In epistolam Iohannis ad Parthos, *Tract. VII.8; PL 35:2033; SCh 75: 75:328.*

**Augustine,* Tractatus in Iohannem *51.10; PL 35:1767; CC 36:443.*

You must have the charity of an angel, opening your arms in love to those who insult and defame you. Like the camp which came to the help of Elisha in his struggles,* you must take care never to repay them evil for evil.* No, if the maidens are hungry, give them food, and strive to defeat evil by good.* This is the glory of the battle camp of heaven, this is the battle array of that host, for it is then alone that charity truly shows herself as victor, when she has overthrown the foe by acts of kindness and turned the hostile forces into friends. This is the way to become a fellow citizen of those heavenly citizens that you have tried to imitate. Now you are marching with them, arrayed for victory, then you will be arrayed with them for glory.

Cf. 2 Kgs 7

Cf. Ps 7:4

Cf. Pr 25:21

11. But since this sermon requires to be concluded, let us turn in prayer to the spouse, the only Son of the Father. In his goodness, may he lavish on us the blessings with which he has so generously blessed his bride, he who, with the same Father and the Holy Spirit, is God, blessed above all that is, for ever and ever.

Amen.

SERMON FORTY-EIGHT

The beginning of the forty-eighth sermon. Of the bride's bodily eye first, which she is bidden to turn away so that spiritual sight may ensue; or next, which is more likely, that this command seems only to be said in the fashion of lovers: the spouse is testing the bride, and does not mean her to obey him.

'TURN YOUR EYES away from me,
Sg 6:4 for they make me fly away.'*
Ps 92:1 'It is good to confess to the Lord,'*
good to praise him, good to bless him. For the
man who confesses has a very great reward, that
the Son will also confess him before his Fa-
Cf. Mt 10:32 ther,* and the man who has God's praise always
Cf. Ps 34:1 on his lips,* his soul will be praised by the
Lord, and Solomon tells us that 'the soul that
Pr 11:25 blesses, is enriched with blessings.'* The bride
knows all this very well, and pours herself out
in confessing, praising and blessing her spouse.
She confesses, praises and blesses him before
the angels of God, also, and finally, even be-
Cf. Mt 6:9 fore her spouse's Father, who is in heaven.*

Obviously, the confession she makes to the daughters of Jerusalem, telling them the secret of the love with which she is aflame for her beloved, is not prompted by loose-lipped talkativeness, but only by a burning charity for her sisters. She is not seeking her own glory, but is yearning to save the souls of others. The holy angels are witness to the complete purity of her intention, for they see everything she is doing, and the bride hopes that they will be her mediators and guides to bring her actions to the end she desires. Furthermore, she has anchored her whole hope in the Father of the Word. She hopes that he will reveal himself to her, and she prays to his only Son, the only one who reveals him, to whomever he chooses.* *Cf. Mt 11:27*

2. So the bride, eager with desire for the blessing of the spirit, blesses her beloved with every blessing she knows, and, as she expected, she bears back now, from her beloved, blessings in exchange. Although there is no simple case of 'exchange', when the one who has done nothing more than bless is overwhelmed with the blessings of the other. It is all too true what scripture tells us of the spouse, 'May everyone who blesses you, overflow with blessings.'* For his part, he receives a *Gen 27:29* blessing, but 'he who is God, blessed above all things for ever,'* does not 'overflow' with the *Rom 31:9* blessings we can give him! 'I am full',* he says, *Cf. Is 1:11* 'and though all the rivers of benediction, whether human or angelic, may run 'into the sea, the sea does not overflow'.* But when he *Sir 1:7* opens his hand and stretches it out to bless, then, as scripture says, 'he fills all creatures with his benediction'.* So the bride offers a *Ps 145:16* simple blessing and receives in return a great weight of blessing. For her, to be blessed means to be made holy, and to be praised means to accept from her spouse an increase of grace.

3. First, then, the spouse has commended the bride for her unusually striking beauty, sweetness and comeliness, and next, for her awe-inspiring gravity. It is as if he has begun with these qualities, using them to introduce and preface his panegyric, as if, raising his eyes first to the eyes of his beloved, he uses them as his starting point. 'Turn your eyes away from me,' he says, 'for they make me
Sg 6:4 fly away.'* Now, taken at their face value, these words of praise have more a note of censure than of approval. They sound very much like a curse, but not at all like a blessing! What can we make of them? Surely this is a terrible curse, to be told to turn her eyes away from the one sole person she desires to look upon? Why not rather tell her to pluck them out, for she could far more easily do without them than keep them from gazing at her beloved? And is not this note of censure heavily underlined, since they make the beloved 'fly away', openly proclaiming that he finds them a stumbling block, as if she were staring at him with a passionate curiosity, more than is fitting or becoming?

Cf. Jn 6:63 But the literal meaning, which 'kills'* the enemies of the Word, cannot do any harm to the bride. From the Spirit of her beloved, which she has received, she has learned how to hear and understand the language of love, a language even higher than that of angels. In fact, she has learned how to speak it to the spouse and, as far as seems called for, about him. It is not difficult to understand these words as referring to that newly won bride to whom, so we read, the spouse in the very flower of his youth was betrothed, for his final words, as he hastened back to that place whence he came to us, bore some resemblance to the words under consideration. For the spouse tells us himself, 'I am telling you the truth, it is for your good that I should go. If I do not go away, the Paraclete will not come to you.'* *Cf. Hos 2:15* *Jn 16:7*

4. Why is it difficult to believe that even then, he used these same words to his same bride: 'Turn your eyes away from me, for they make me fly away'?* While still satisfied to look at him merely with her bodily eyes, these eyes were a great and painful stumbling-block to her. Rather, she must turn them away, she must drop them, so that, when he flies away to the Father, her eyes may take wing also, and fly away by his side. There they will grow accustomed to a new light and marvel to find themselves receiving a new keenness of vision, no longer tormented by his bodily absence, rather delighting in the sight of Christ their Lord become Spirit. To say, then, 'Turn your eyes away from me', means nothing more than: lay aside your worldly way of looking, and change eyes tender as doves, that keep you cleaving to my bodily presence, for eyes stronger than those of eagles. And indeed, these eyes are full of grace, having their due praise in the past, when the bride was still weak. For the marvelous sweetness of living close to Jesus made all the glory of this world appear in their sight like withered grass of the meadow.* This is why, in days gone by, it was perhaps right for the bride to hear the admiring, 'Your eyes are *Sg 6:4* *Cf. Is 40:7*

Sg 1:14 doves' eyes.'* These are eyes of true gentleness and innocence, but they are over-ingenuous and not very sharp-sighted. There is no longer place for them. A time was when the bride profited greatly from knowing Christ in his bodily form, but now, something far higher has been prepared for her by her
2 Cor 5:16 spouse.*

5. So, if you will allow me, these words should be taken as referring to that early
Cf. Bernard, SC 8.2; SBOp 1.37; CF 4:46. church, who is the mother of us all, and what joy it is that all the fullness of love
Cf. Col 1:19 should dwell within her. To the extent that she has been able to become the possession of perfect lovers, in this sense this phrase will bear the meaning we have discussed. But if, on the other hand, this same phrase is to be applied to any soul you like, who has drunk deep of the same Spirit and so all the more
Cf. Sir 24:29 strongly thirsts for him still,* then, 'even as the hart longs for the streams of water, so
Ps 42:1 she longs'* and thirsts for 'God, the living
Ps 42:2 stream'*. She cannot satisfy her thirst until she comes and appears before the face of
Ibid. God,* for it is he, the living stream, that can fill the thirsting soul. If it is a soul like this we have in mind, the meaning of the phrase will still be much the same.

This soul too, will hasten, by the identical stages, towards the end she has set before her, which is perfection, the fullness of charity, and she will pursue, and go on pursuing, until she lays hold of it. And we must not think she at once reaches the goal of perfection, either. No, she has been reared in its first principles, and from the earliest years of her childhood, she has been trained by her loving nurse, the Lord Jesus. Then, when she had matured to riper years, she was handed over to the Holy Spirit, so that he himself might teach her. For, as Jesus said to his first friends, 'The Holy Spirit, whom the Father will send in my name, he it is who will teach you everything, and bring to your minds everything that I have said to you.'* *Jn 15:26*

Indeed, he is the very Spirit of love, the fount of charity, the living stream; it is he who creates new eyes for those who would see Jesus, by illuminating their minds and enkindling their hearts. Accordingly, in every soul that the Spirit has anointed with the oil of gladness,* so that it may desire Jesus, he *Ps 45:8* accomplishes his end in the same manner. And the result is that the bodily way of acting, whether in thought or affection, the way in which, while the soul was still an inexperienced young girl, she eagerly clung to the spouse of her youth, gradually and little by little, turns into a strength that is all spiritual.

6. The Truth knows nothing of lies, but he gives weight to his proclamation of the truth, all the same, and says to us, 'I am telling you the truth, it is for your good that I am going away.'* If it had not been the Truth *Jn 16:7* himself, who cannot deny what he is,* who *Cf. Jn 14:6* told us with his own lips that it was good for us that he should go away and leave us without him for the time being, who would believe it? Who would not immediately recoil, or shrink back as from some blasphemous utterance? Nevertheless, on the lips of Truth himself, this is how the fullness of charity was

fittingly portrayed, that fullness which was to be poured forth into the hearts of his dear
Cf. Rom 5:5 ones through the Holy Spirit.* He wanted his repeated promise to make our inmost heart wide open in expectation, and then he wanted a longing for him to expand our heart into
Cf. Mt 9:17 new wineskins to receive new wine.* For 'no one', as Jesus says, 'puts new wine into old
Mk 2:22 wineskins,'* in case the wineskins are destroyed and the wine runs out, or else the wine bursts the skins, and again the wine is lost and the skins destroyed.

But here we have a new fullness of the Spirit coming upon us, and that requires stronger eyes. Therefore the spouse speaks to the soul who loves him tenderly but in a bodily fashion, being still taken up with the bodily consideration of Christ's flesh, and he
Sg 6:4 tells her, 'Turn your eyes away from me,'* because, as he says himself, 'it is the Spirit
Jn 6:64 that gives life, the flesh profits us nothing.'* Learn to see me spiritually, learn to taste me spiritually, no longer clinging to the breasts, but seated at the right hand of my Father. When my disciples love me in the flesh, it 'makes me fly away', for fear that, if I stay with them any longer, I will never make them perfect, since I am not allowing them to be weaned. Your eyes, also, have 'made me fly away', for though you have already been weaned, it is time now to long for the things of heaven, and to gaze on the spiritual realities that belong to me.

In this sense then, these words can be applied either to the church or to any soul that truly loves God.

7. But I have been thinking deeply about this phrase, and it has not been difficult to persuade myself that it was not said with the authority of one who gives commands, but rather with a disposition to suggest or test. This is how nearly everything that the spouse says in the song seems to be addressed to the bride, as though he were asking her or bringing something to her mind, rather than ordering her. It is in this tone he seems to say, 'Show me your face, let your voice sound in my ears.'* And in just the same way, 'Open to me, my sister, my love, my dove, my perfect one, for my head is wet with dew, and my locks with the drops of night.'* So much are these words of entreaty and not of command, that the bride appears slow in granting his requests. In fact, we hear words of excuse, that she will find it troublesome to rise, because she has taken off her robe and washed her feet.* In this song, it seems to me, you will discover the spouse very frequently speaking in this tone, so that the unmistakable impression is of a tender feeling of love, which ought to be implied rather than commanded, drawn out by an affectionate coaxing rather than elicited by stern decrees.

Sg 2:14

Sg 5:2

Cf. Sg 5:3

8. I read, too, in the gospel, how the Lord of glory asked Simon Peter to push out a little from the shore in his boat.* But his voice was the voice that Moses once heard, not commanding but almost as though appealing and calling to mind: 'Leave me alone, that my anger may blaze against this people.'* Certainly Moses had the courage to take no heed of this remark, while he would never

Cf. Lk 5:3

Ex 32:10

have dared to resist a definite command. In the same way, we read that the angel said to Jacob, 'Leave me alone, for the dawn is
Gen 32:26 upon us.'* But Jacob resisted him confidently, because the angel was merely asking or hinting, and he did not allow him to be parted from him until he had first obtained, or
Cf. Gen 32:26 rather, extorted, a blessing.* And there is another instance in Elijah, when he was vehemently demanding that Elisha leave him alone. He heard Elisha answer: 'As the Lord lives,
2 Kgs 2:2 and as you live, I will not leave you.'* This disobedience on the part of his disciple caused the master no displeasure at all, though he opposed him once, twice and a third time. There was far more delight in seeing him react as a friend, with loving sorrow, not allowing the sweet bond between them to be broken.

It is very probable that what the spouse wants here is to receive from his bride some repulse like this. This may well be why he says to her, 'Turn, for they make me fly
Sg 6:4 away.'* Clearly, when he told Moses, 'Leave
Ex 32:10 me alone, that my anger may blaze,'* his real intention was certainly not to be obeyed, for he permitted him to resist him, as well as
Cf. Ex 32:14 persuade him to change his mind.* God was speaking to his servant, yet not treating him as a servant, but speaking in the usual way a
Cf. Ex 53:11 man will speak to his friend.* In the same way, he invested him with that trustful intimacy which enabled him to reply, not in the usual way of servant to master, but of friend to friend. So he brought forward many powerful reasons, and at length called his

heart back from the revenge on which he was determined. With his counsels of moderation, he imposed a bridle on his wrath, and so proved himself a true friend, for obeying the laws of friendship, he did not allow his friend in a fury to pursue his own will. And the one who wrestled with Jacob and said to him, 'Leave me alone',* really wanted to be held tight rather than left alone, because it was obviously he who strengthened Jacob in soul and body so that he could hold him and not 'leave him alone'.

Gen 32:26

I think this is what is happening here, that the spouse is speaking to his bride as friend speaks to friend. Every now and then, as is the way of lovers, he makes some suggestion which he is pleased should not be obeyed, especially since what he says implies the possibility of separation.

9. For what forebearance could enable the bride even to hear, 'Turn your eyes away from me'?* Clearly, in what follows, 'they make me fly away', it seems to me that purity of intention and serenity of mind are being praised by the spouse, and that in contemplating the beauty of the beloved the bride is flourishing in these virtues. Yes, the bride is blessed indeed to be 'pure of heart',* for it is the purity of her intention that makes her fit for the vision of her spouse.* Yet she is still more blessed in the deeper serenity of mind which has made her fit already, not just to see God one day, but to see him here and now.* The simple eye of a loving intention makes the whole body of a good deed light,* which would have been full of darkness

Sg 6:4

Cf. Mt 5:8

Cf. Gilbert, SC *30.3; PL 184:156; CF 20:364.*

Cf. Job 19:26

Cf. Mt 6:22

if it had not been illuminated with this light here on earth. But now, all lit up by the light of this eye, the whole of the good deed can become a lamp of splendor, even able to give light to the very intention which filled it with light in the first place. All the same, though, the eye of the mind is even more luminous, because it is able to transform the soul that contemplates God into that same image, and to carry it forward from brightness into brightness.*

Cf. 2 Cor 3:18

It was this eye that the spouse meant when he said to the bride, earlier in the poem, 'You have wounded my heart with one of your eyes.'* Strong and piercing is the gaze of the understanding,* which has been able, not merely to penetrate the very heart of the Word, but even to wound it. 'Someone has touched me',* said Jesus, because of a woman who believed and, through faith, was rewarded by being cleansed from her flow of blood.* So it is good to touch him, and draw strength from the fringe of his garment, but far more effective to strike him with the stroke of love and violently wrest grace from the heart of the one we have wounded. So it is a wounded spouse who 'flies away', and he takes his flight to the heights, so that he may carry away with him the eyes of the beloved that have wounded him, and satisfy them to the full with a more sublime sight. Should I say 'satisfy' them, or 'wound' them? He has suffered being wounded by the bride, and now, in his turn, he does not forget to wound her in return and, as scripture says, 'to slay her with wound upon wound'.*

Sg 4:9

Cf. Gilbert, SC *18.4; PL 184:94; CF 20:231.*

Lk 8:46

Cf. Lk 8:44

Cf. Job 16:15

The spouse, then, 'flies away', but not in order to leave the bride behind him. No, he wants her to become like the eagle that is flying to and fro above her,* he wants her to *Cf. Deut 32:11*
learn how to take wing and, wherever he should fly, to strive to fly after him and to him. For where can he fly that she cannot follow?* And as far as her strength holds out, *Cf. Ps 139:7*
she will at least follow him with her eyes. Even if he goes up to heaven and there shuts himself up in his Father's bosom,* and stays *Cf. Jn 1:18*
there, the Word in his beginning, as he has been from the beginning,* even there, through *Cf. Jn 1:1*
lattices and chinks, as far as she can, the bride will cleave to her beloved.* She will trace him *Cf. Sg 6:3*
by the fragrance of his perfume.* *Cf. Sg 1:3*

So, when she hears from her spouse that she is to 'turn her eyes away', it seems to her that these words are really meant to test her, to see whether, even when it is he himself who suggests it, she will submit to turning them away from him. If she does, she will show herself to be, in this respect, less ardent in love than Jacob or Moses or Elijah, who rejected, in the spirit of freedom, any suggestion of this nature. For love gives courage to freedom, as if love has the courage to withstand God from the very quality that makes it true to him, as God himself has told us.* *Cf. Jn 8:32*
Otherwise, to obey the beloved in this matter would be the same as if seeming to stop loving him.

For how could her heart not be 'where her treasure is', and her eyes also?* Surely the *Cf. Mt 6:21*
bride would be right to reply and tell him: Where can my eyes look, if I may not look at

you? Would you have me numbered among the foolish virgins, who, precisely for this very reason, that they do not look on you, are forced 'to look at vain and empty falsehoods'?* And this is why, poor, wretched creatures, their lamps will be found without light, when you appear.* In the present life they have no longing to be your bride, and they do not keep their eyes upon your beauty, and so, in the time to come, they will not be able to go out to meet you as you draw near, or follow after as you return.

Ps 40:5

Cf. Mt 25:2

10. Never let it happen, Lord my God, O, never let it happen, my beloved, that the gaze of my eyes be fixed anywhere but on my Head, so that I may cleave without intermission to you, my beloved. Wherever you go, or whenever you fly away, I shall make every effort I can to follow you, and when I cannot catch up with you, I shall be happy to follow on until I faint.* These words are constantly in my mind: 'As the Lord lives, and as I live, I shall not let you alone,'* but my eyes will always be on you.* Whatever my Lord commands me, I am ready to obey, happy to be your handmaid, but that you should turn your eyes away from me, or I my eyes from you, that is something I cannot bear to hear. No, rather you must turn your eyes to me, and mine to you, for I will never be able to look on you, unless you first look on me, most Beautiful, most Powerful, most Sweet, only Son of the Father, with Him, and the Holy Spirit, you live and reign, God, for ever and ever. Amen.

Cf. Phil 3:12

2 Kgs 4:30

Cf. Ps 25:14

SERMON FORTY-NINE

The beginning of the forty-ninth sermon. How the hair of the spouse, which is compared to goats, stands for those who have the appearance of holiness in the church. How, for any soul that loves God, this kind of hair symbolizes thoughts of humility, which their own weakness brings to their assistance.

'YOUR HAIR IS LIKE a flock of goats, which appear from Gilead.'* *Sg 6:4*

After praising the eyes, from whose serene gaze the spouse declares that he 'has flown away', we move on to celebrate the hair. In the human body, of course, hair holds a more eminent position than the eyes do, but as far as ability, beauty and usefulness go, it is worth far less. Indeed, regarding the outer husk of this phrase, it makes very meagre and arid reading, so that Israel 'according to the flesh',* whose share is nothing but this outer husk, tastes it and does not find it sweet. He eats it, and it does him no good. Thanks be to the Lord our God, that he has settled us on 'the high places of the earth'* where he could give us 'the inheritance of Jacob'* for our food! He has given understanding to his little ones,* so that they have learned to suck 'honey from the rock, and oil from the flinty crag',* and to eat 'goats with

1 Cor 10:18

Cf. Deut 32:13

Deut 32:9

Cf. Lk 10:21

Deut 32:13

Deut 32:14 the finest of wheat'.* At this point, when we, too, have goat set before us as our meal, may the Spirit be with us, putting beside us 'the finest of wheat'.

2. The goat, as we know, is a wanton animal, ugly and rank, that destroys the tender shoots of the trees. To my mind, goats symbolize the wantonness of the impure, whose lot, at the last day, will be to stand on
Cf. Mt 25:33 the left hand.* The shepherd's staff will separate from one another those whom we now see all feeding indiscriminately together on the mountains of Israel, and that day will show us an unforgettable sight. From then on, the lambs will pasture as befits them, and the kids will be separated off, equally as is
Cf. Mt 25:32 fitting.* Oh, what a peal of thunder! Oh, how terrible it will be, the voice of the shepherd cursing his beast and cutting it off for ever
Cf. Mt 25:41 from his sheepfold!* For on that day, there will be nothing in common between the spotless Lamb, and the aggressive and spotted, between the beautiful and the ugly, between the one who is the fragrance of life that leads to life, and the other, who is the stench of
Cf. 2 Cor 2:16 death that leads to death.* There will be no common ground for the one who plants and
Cf. 1 Cor 3:7 waters and gives the increase,* and the one who devours and wreches away and squanders.

3. But, you will say, what likeness or comparison can there be between the bride and flocks of this kind of goat? In every way she is different from them, pure, fragrant and lovely as she is. Yet her spouse has already
Sg 2:2 praised her for being 'a lily among thorns',* for it is among maidens of this kind that she

flowers, and living in their midst she preserves her whiteness and her perfume most marvelously and graciously. And from the very pricking of these thorns, think what patience she derives, what gentleness, wisdom, humility and grace! To live always with the angels will be a supreme and overwhelming happiness for the holy and sinless bride, in other words, to be a lily among lilies, but from the thorns she certainly draws the glory of greater virtue. They are ruined themselves, and they ruin everything that they possess, yet the bride not only suffers no loss of holiness from contact with them, she actually grows in grace. So these lilies live in the midst of thorns of this nature, in order to increase in grace, and in addition, their blooming shows the thorns what sanctity is like. And when, on the other hand, they are pricked by the thorns, this gives them occasion to rejoice with their spouse and say, 'They repaid me evil for good',* 'they hated me without *Ps 35:12*
cause.'* *Jn 15:25*

4. Therefore, among the many who draw near the bride, there are some of this nature, who are, as it were, 'hairs', that veil and cover her head, since they adorn and strengthen her mind with a mantle of different virtues. For what other reason except necessity can make it inevitable for scandals to come,* for *Cf. Mt 18:7*
heresies to arise, for battles and discords to take place, for sin to abound and love to grow cold?* Why else should ambition run *Cf. Mt 24:12*
wild in today's church with such an excess of impudent freedom, so that she casts far away from her all veil of modesty, and foul

disease consumes every part of her body? 'From the sole of her foot to the crown of her
Is 1:16 head',* there is little health left in her. Every evil like this seems to be, as Solomon says, like an error that proceeds from the
Cf. Qo 10:5 prince's presence.* Exhaustively to investigate the real reasons why all these things will be a labor that will only end when you
Ps 73:16 'enter the sanctuary of God'* and see for yourself that everything is being done for the wellbeing of the bride. She is God's charge,
Cf. 1 Pet 5:7 His alone.*

Clearly enough, the bride lets her spouse send her persecutors so as to strengthen her in perseverance, heretics to instruct her in wisdom, men without purity to exercise her in purity. She receives the unjust so as to defend justice more strongly, those enamoured of the belly so as to fight with greater vigor for the virtue of temperance, the proud and rebellious to teach her humility and meekness, the impatient and the stern to test her in gentleness and patience, and, finally, the disdain and violence of the ambitious to rouse her up to practice holy poverty. In short, all the wickedness of evil-doers is for her a furnace and a file and a hammer. She uses it to burn out of her whatever is impure, to file down whatever is rough, to get rid of whatever is disfiguring, to give form to whatever is formless, and to bring into line whatever is out of keeping. Have we not here, quite
Cf. Mt 13:55 truly, 'the carpenter's son'?* For he knows how to make contraries produce the likeness of their contraries, how to bring health out of infirmities, and from vices to form

virtues and give them practice.

So it was as a veil, as the apostle says,* that hair like this was given to this woman, to the bride of God who is the church. They are coarse and bristly hairs, not much in keeping with the elegance of such great beauty, but for the time being, they are necessary. Indeed, she has another head of hair, very different from this and much more noble, namely, the pre-eminent strength of her virtue, which the spouse praises in his heart. For later on in the song, he says, 'The locks of your head are like the purple robes of a king, joined together in their tresses.'* *Cf. 1 Cor 11:15* *Sg 7:5*

5. You will notice that this commendation sounds very unlike the other, and it is perhaps significant that he has spoken in one place of 'locks' and in the other of 'hair'. There it is described as 'purple', suggesting the graceful uniformity of a head of hair, seen as a whole. Here, the hairs are compared to 'a flock of goats', hinting at the great diversity of the wicked who disturb her. Hence comes that cry of lamentation, 'More numerous than the hairs of my head are those who hate me without cause.'* Indeed, very true are the words used elsewhere of those hairs which, like purple, adorn the bride's head for all eternity. Not one of them will perish,* precisely because now they have all been numbered,* and no one is able to diminish that number in the slightest. *Ps 69:4* *Cf. Lk 21:18* *Cf. Mt 10:30*

But these other hairs, 'whose number cannot be counted',* are not hastening to be of that blessed number. And in consequence, this hair will not be able to weigh down the *Ps 40:6*

bride's head for long, for it is hair that belongs to this world. Although, in the sight of her spouse and his holy angels, she is adorned and crowned by it, nevertheless, on the last day, it will be to her a distress and a burden beyond all bearing. Listen, then, to what kind of judgement hair like this will receive on that last day, and even on this present day, too. 'Take a sharp sword,' says the Lord to the prophet, 'use it as a barber's razor, and pass it over your head and your beard; then take balances for weighing, and divide the hair. A third part you shall burn in the fire in the center of the city; and a third part you shall take and strike with the sword round about the city; and a third part you shall scatter to the wind, and I will unsheathe the sword after them. And you shall take from these a small number, and bind them in the skirts of your robe. And of these again you shall take some, and cast them into the fire, and burn them in the fire; from there a fire will come
Ez 5:1-4 forth into all the house of Israel.'*

That sword, sharpened so finely that it can shave off, not only the hair of the head, but even the hairs of the body, what is it if not the sword of God's judgement, in so far as that is both discriminating and penetrating? Quite apart from the intentions that come from deliberate consideration, it is both able and willing to sift the value of even the instinctive motion of the flesh or the idle intentions of the heart. So sharp is it that it is described as
Cf. Zech 9:14 like a flash of lightning,* for it pierces through all that is closed, it reveals all that is hidden, it irradiates all that is dark.

6. This is the sword that the Son of man is told to take and draw over his head and his beard.* It is to the virgin's Son that this judgement belongs, for to him it was given,* and the evil men who preside over the church, as if weighing down her head, as well as the evil men who cling to it, as if disfiguring her face, he is ordered to kill and shave away with his discriminating justice. Moreover, the unsearchable depth of the wisdom of God,* which is the most just balance of his judgements, orders that the balance should come into the hands of him to whom it belongs by right, so that, with perfect order, he can give every individual man the exact measure of punishment that he deserves. It will be his office to weigh the matter of merits and the diversities of gifts, and from this he will discover what vessels are fitted for what destruction. Isaiah prophesied that a plumbline of perdition should be stretched out even to the earth,* so that, by a cord that can make a most just distribution, that inheritance too, should be divided among his heirs.*

Cf. Ez 5:1
Cf. Jn 5:22
Cf. Rom 11:33
Cf. Is 34:11
Cf. Ps 78:56

7. It follows, then, from what Ezekiel says, that the sons of wrath will be separated from one another into three parts and each will receive the punishment that is deserved. A third part will be burnt by fire in the midst of the city, a third will be struck with a sword round about the city, and a third will be scattered to the wind and the sword will be unsheathed after them.* Quite clearly, a large part of them will be consumed by the heat of bodily lust, while a part no smaller will be given over to stealing and struggling, and will

Cf. Ez 5:2

be cut off by the sword of anger and envy and hatred. Then the part that remains, putting forth every effort to swallow down the empty air of vain glory, will be completely whirled away on the wind of ambition.

The first will perish 'in the midst of the city', that is, in the sight of all. Obviously, by living together, and spurring one another on by advice and example, they have, as it were, conspired among themselves to set the whole city on fire. But the second group will be slain 'round about the city', and this is the reason: those who run greedily after earthly wealth, roam around with their minds eagerly intent upon seeking men to devour, and means of devouring them,* determined to glut on them their hunger. And we must not pass carelessly over the last group, those whom we are told will have a sword unsheathed after them, and whom we hear of as being ordered to be scattered to the wind. What can we be meant to understand by the sword that is 'unsheathed after them', if not the power that has been usurped by them? It is well said that 'it will be unsheathed after them', when it is drawn out, by the hand of the all-powerful judge, from the sheath of a false security, so that the very sword which they used to destroy their subjects and condemn themselves, may now pursue them and strike them down. Of course, as far as concerns the ministry of teaching, which they have undertaken, this sword holds its peace within its scabbard, giving offense to no one by refuting cover appealing to conscience or rebuking sin. Only to acquire some

Cf. 1 Pet 5:8

advantage will it be drawn from the sheath. But the Son of man is coming, yes, he is coming, and he will bare this sword. He will string it free of its plunder, he will denude it of its dignities, he will strip it of its subterfuges, and over the heads of the haughty, he will brandish it. Then all who have taken the sword, will perish by the sword they have taken.* *Cf. Mt 26:52*

8. A small part of them are to be 'bound into the skirts of his robe',* which means very clearly that section of the church which is enthroned on the highest seat of power. The 'skirt of the robe' is the first and highest distinction of ecclesiastical authority, the glory of kingly and priestly dignity, woven with most beautiful ornamentation. When Jesus, our Elijah, ascended into heaven, it was this robe that he left to his apostles and their representatives, to console them for his absence and to be a mantle for his church.* Let them take care that what they have received for the glory of God and the protection of God's bride, should not be misappropriated into a coverlet for their own honor, leaving the church in her nakedness. For my part, I have said this with fear and trembling, 'but the Word of God is not bound.'* The Spirit says clearly, for all to hear, that from the hairs that have been 'bound into the skirts of the robe', a 'fire will go forth into all the house of Israel'.* It is not my desire to dwell upon the interpretation of these things, but the foundations of the earth will be shaken* and the pillars of heaven will tremble,* at the voice of the

Cf. Ez 5:3
Cf. 2 Kgs 2:13
2 Tim 2:9
Ez 5:4
Cf. Ps 18:7
Cf. Job 26:11

Lord God of hosts.

And all this has been said in reference to those hairs of the bride which are compared by the spouse to 'a flock of goats, which appear from Gilead',* so that the summit of Gilead may be understood as being the highest point in the church, which a little while before I spoke of as symbolized by 'the skirts of the robe'.

Cf. Sg 6:4

9. Most certainly, Gilead has every right to be called the 'church of the godly', seeing that the very word 'Gilead' means 'a heap of witness',* a pile built up only of chosen stones into a mound of 'covenant',† raised up on high to become a lofty mountain. So it is 'a heap', because of the great number of stones or witnesses, and it is 'a mound of witness or covenant', because the witnesses are all united, since what the heart believes, the lips are quick to speak, when the critical moment arrives and demands it. The church confirms the testimony of her lips by the evidence of her works, so that she may truly be, and truly be called 'the witness of Israel', who rises up 'to confess the name of the Lord',* to be as true a witness in heaven as she has been on earth.*

**Cf. Gen 31:47. This is the translation of Gilead given by St Jerome in his* Book on the Interpretation of Hebrew Names.

†Cf. Gen 31:48

Cf. Ps 122:4

Cf. Ps 89:36

Yet it is from this mountain that 'the flocks of goats' appear, simultaneously with the sheep, but they do no more than 'appear', and they 'appear' only for a short time. In fact, they are not said 'to appear', but rather, 'to have appeared', because from the viewpoint of eternity a vapor appearing is as if it had no reality; it scarcely comes into being before it has ceased to be. There have appeared, then, on mount Gilead, these flocks of goats interspersed with flocks of sheep, and from that mountain, they show themselves to the Great Shepherd, who stands among his animals and says, 'Behold, I am the judge between one animal and another.'* *Ez 34:17*

The holiness of the elect makes the sinfulness of the wicked among whom they live, seem ever more degraded, and to be cheek by jowl with goodness shows up the full degradation of the base of heart. It is well said, then, that 'they have appeared from Gilead', because what they truly are is shown very clearly by the comparison with the just. Obviously, they have no right to say, 'Gilead is mine',* since they do no more than *Ps 60:7* 'appear from mount Gilead'. They do not belong now to mount Gilead, for their actions give the lie to what their lips proclaim.

10. On the other hand, if these same words are applied to one soul only, she who has entered the marriage couch of the spouse and been anointed with the royal chrism, that she may worthily be known by the title of queen and bride, having upon her head the crown of the kingdom, then these words must bear another meaning, though one that is not totally different. Naturally, she has also beautifully arranged her hair, desiring to give pleasure to her spouse, not 'with elaborate braiding',* as the apostle calls it, *1 Tim 2:9* deceiving her spouse's eyes, but doing all she can to be conformed to him by her most lowly thoughts and desires, in the way she has learnt from the master of humility himself. This makes her very anxious to increase

greatly in humility, for from this she will win herself great beauty. The humbler she can become, the more beautiful she will appear to her spouse, and so she multiplies all the various reasons why she has cause to be humble, as if they were countless 'flocks of goats' in her own regard. She passes carefully in review all her own deformities, singing
David humbly with him* who is father to the
Cf. Mt 1:6 Word, according to the flesh:* 'My iniquities have laid hold of me, so that I cannot see. They are more numerous than the hairs of
Ps 40:15 my head.'*

See how the many flocks of goats are likened to the number of her hairs, and how they make the bride all the more rich in adornment, the more she herself feels her poverty and thinks little of her own beauty. Not only her former sins, but any part of herself still sullied by some defect or groping in ignorance, any part lying fallow because of her neglect in the cultivation of virtue, all these things she holds up to her gaze, and she feels no shame in thrusting them upon her spouse's attention. With amazing skill, she strives to give him pleasure by the very things which have caused her to find displeasure in herself!

It follows that these 'flocks of goats' form a rich source of wealth for the bride, and though she may have a rank smell, it is for this very reason that her spouse finds her fragrant. In her own eyes, she wounds herself with cause for compunction, and this is what makes her wound her spouse to the heart with cause for love. For the wounded spouse says, 'You have wounded my heart, my sister, my bride, you have wounded my heart with one glance of your eyes, with one hair of your neck'.* From one of her eyes and from one hair of her neck, as from a twofold arrow, the spouse has received a twofold wound in his heart. The bride looks with delight at the beauty of her spouse, fixing the thoughts of her mind serenely upon him, but nevertheless, at the same time, she considers herself to be only one of the goats, a poor thing in her own judgement of herself.* In the eyes of her spouse, this makes her very lovable, since by such a combination of qualities she preserves intact this gift of both these graces.

Sg 4:9

**Cf. Bernard,* Hum *I.2; SBOp 3:17; CF 13:30-1.*

11. Moreover, it is very fitting that the verse should go on to say that these 'flocks of goats' 'have appeared from Gilead'. The heaping up of humble thoughts indeed forms a 'mound', and there is nothing more efficacious than a mound to reinforce the witness of a good conscience. Obviously, nothing can so purge the whole conscience absolutely clean, clear it to absolute clarity, cleanse it to absolute sinlessness, than the meticulous getting rid of anything unworthy and 'the appeal to God for a good conscience',* as the apostle Peter calls it. Any soul that has become accustomed to this, can truly say with pride, 'Gilead is mine'.* I repeat, any one who has learnt to accept his weakness and deformity, not as a goad of dishonor, but as a spur to heaping up the honor of humility, can say honestly, 'Gilead is mine'. And she will hear from her spouse that these flocks of goats have appeared from Gilead, so that it may be 'a

1 Pet 3:21

Ps 60:7

mound of witness' between God and the soul. It will witness that the things she deliberately used to become dissatisfied with herself, ought not, from now on, make God dissatisfied with her, and that God ought not to use in evidence against her the things she has not scrupled to use against herself.

So, these flocks appear; they appear to the judge that is conscience; they appear, too, to the judge that is God. But, they appear 'from Gilead', namely, from the witness of a good conscience. Therefore, since in the presence of God, she does not spare herself, her conscience bears its witness and absolves
Cf. Ps 7:12 her. God 'who judges justly',* not only does not judge the one who judges herself, but makes her beautiful and glorious because of the very things that made the soul displeased with itself. For this is how the most just of judges and the most loving of judges 'judges
Cf. Ps 71:2 his poor with justice',* and above all others, judges his beloved, on whose beauty his eyes rest day and night. And this is his verdict: whatever men have first condemned in themselves, they will not be condemned for again. On the contrary, they will not only receive pardon for these things, but grace and glory also.

12. From what has been said, it can very easily be seen that this commendation does not come from men, but from God. These words cannot be of human invention, for the human ear would shrink from hearing them, did not the Spirit, who utters them, stand behind them. It is indisputable, therefore, that they come from heaven, for they would

otherwise be altogether harsh and grating. What the spouse is praising, then, in the hair of his beloved, which he likens to flocks of goats, is her profound humility. So her locks are far more to be admired than the hair of Samson, strongest of men, in that they have taught her not to have anything to do with false Delilah.* It is precisely this arrogance, this self-satisfaction, whose 'speech is smoother than oil',* that is all-powerful in laying hold of souls, especially those who trust in their own strength.* No false woman has more power than she, and it is tragic to think how many men, men of outstanding quality, she has lulled to sleep in her lap. She has shorn their locks and put out their eyes and so doomed them in the end to slave labor at the mill of fleshly toil. Then they have the shame of seeing themselves cast down from a throne of glory and bound to the narrow circle of the mill.*

Cf. Jdg 16

Pr 5:3

Cf. Ps 47:6

Cf. Jdg 16:21

The spouse consequently protects his beloved from this bane of great souls and sees to the hairs of her head, not one of which the razor of flattery or the craft of secret pride will be able to cut off. For she is entrenched in a deeply rooted humility and invincible to her enemies because of the invisible strength of her hair. In the exceptional beauty of that hair, she shows herself to her spouse, worthy of the love of the Son of God, who together with the Father and the Holy Spirit,

lives and reigns, God,
for ever and ever.
Amen.

SERMON FIFTY

The beginning of the fiftieth sermon. How these words of praise are directed towards those who are rightly zealous for the church. They feed on her as if they were teeth, and nevertheless, despite their positions of authority, by the virtue of humility, they are part of the flock, as it were, among all the other sheep. And they bear twins, because they are solicitous for their own salvation and for their brothers'.

'YOUR TEETH are a flock of sheep that have come up from the washing; each one is carrying twins, not one of
Sg 6:5 them is barren.'*

Notice how, to praise his bride, the spouse declaims a second time, in almost exactly the same words, phrases from the previous lines of the song. The only difference is that there
Cf. Sg 4:2 he speaks of a flock of shavelings,* and here of a flock of sheep. But, where praise is concerned, the church has every right to appropriate to herself the leading part, especially since she is the principal object of all the eulogies of this marriage song. Above all else, she claims as her own the glory and the title of queen and bride, so that she has the privilege, in a special way, of saying, 'My
Sg 2:16 beloved is mine, and I am his.'* It is only

right then, that the words we are discussing should first be applied to her.

2. Consequently, in my opinion, the 'teeth of the bud' symbolize those vigorous men who are zealous for her well-being, and who employ themselves in grinding and chewing the food that conduces to the building up of her life and health. For what else but 'teeth' were the holy apostles, and the preachers who are eager to emulate them, whom zeal for our salvation has scattered to the ends of the earth, marking themselves out for death, if only they could win us for Christ?* Surely they were the most hungry of 'teeth', and yet among the sheep, gentleness itself? *Cf. 1 Cor 9:19*

These were clearly men whose ravenous appetite to chew and gnaw, no tribe could meet. No land or kingdom was enough for them, for 'their lines had fallen in pleasant places',* and the salvation of the whole world was to be their food. About this, a very great promise had been made to them: 'You shall eat the wealth of the nations, and in their riches you shall glory.'* For such foods they crave with such insatiable avidity, that they completely disregard any judging or grading of food and think nothing is to be refused, if only they can satisfy their hunger. On the contrary, whatever comes into their hands, they fall upon it with their teeth, too. In fact, it was to one of these preachers that it was said: 'Eat whatever is offered you.'* And this was said to another: 'What God has made clean, you must not call unclean.'* *Ps 16:7* *Is 61:6* *Ez 3:1* *Acts 10:15*

So these are valuable teeth, with a bite that puts paid to the old life, a hunger that prepares for the new life, a greed that makes ready for the life of heaven.

3. But, if we consider the teeth themselves, some among them have the task of cutting off, and are called 'incisors'; some grind and break into pieces, and they are said to be 'canines'; the third group of teeth move round and round, crumbling away, from whence their name of 'molar'. By the same rule, for the same universal Rule-giver is behind it, teeth are arranged in the mouth of the church. The first 'cut off' men to the shape of faith in God and holy fear. Then, with a certain canine and shameless tearing, so to say, they cut asunder what was sordid and unclean. They chew on it, pouring out the new flavor of holiness, so as to fashion it into virtue. Then finally, having schooled them to patience, as if they have now ground them completely down, they make them fit to be received into Christ.

So, if you consider their zeal, there is nothing more biting or voracious than these teeth. But if it is care for the soul you have in mind, there is nothing gentler than they are, nothing more mild. Clearly, when it comes to zeal and enthusiasm, 'they suffered hunger
Ps 59:6 like dogs',* a hunger no less, indeed, than that of the creature of whom it is written,
Job 41:5 'Terror dwells in his rows of teeth.'* Just like that insatiable beast, in fact, which day and night 'prowls around, seeking someone to
1 Pet 5:8 devour,'* so they, in turn, prowl around the city, complaining when they do not find prey
Cf. Ps 59:6 sufficient to content them.* I call it 'complaining', but of course, it is really a holy

kind of complaint, and they are racked with a holy hunger. There was one of them who even desired to be excommunicated for the sake of his brothers, if only they would allow themselves to be eaten by him and incorporated into Christ.* What tooth could be more devouring than this, or rather, what tooth could be more gentle? *Cf. Rom 9:3*

4. Good Jesus, how passionately, and beyond the measure of any human love, charity boiled up in Paul's heart! It was a love that seemed to abandon and disown his own soul, so as to gain the souls of others. Here we truly have teeth 'like a flock of sheep', containing very many of those milk white teeth which scripture refers to: 'His teeth are whiter than milk.'* These teeth are the teeth of the Lord Jesus. He is the most ardent of all those who are zealous for the salvation of mankind, even to the point of being wholly dissatisfied with eating us, unless, in a wonderful and indescribable manner, he too, in his turn, should be eaten by us.* He chews and he swallows and he passes us down into his own self, causing the same hunger within us. He longs to be eaten and tasted, swallowed and united with us, to become most intimately and profoundly a part of us. Hence those loving words of his: 'Make your abode in me, and I in you.'* So what is done in this sacrament of love, when we partake of the body and blood of Christ, is a very clear indication of taking refreshment and internally sharing a meal. It is like a foretaste of the eternal banquet and communion.

Gen 49:12

Cf. Bernard, SC *71.5; SBOp 2:217; CF 40:51-2.*

Jn 15:4

It is a fine description of these teeth,

'whiter than milk', for their whiteness comes from rebuking and correcting, first with a vocal admonition, and then with the whiplash of discipline, and both these flow from loving maternal breasts. This is what scripture means by saying, 'Whom the Lord loves, he corrects,
Pr 3:12 and he whips every son that is dear to him.'* This way of 'correcting' is 'whiter than milk', in that it is sweeter than any human love. Even when it appears to be furiously angry with its sons, this divine love knows nothing of the gloom of real anger, or the unpleasantness of real fury; all it knows is a tranquil love and the white radiance grace brings with it. No, it rebukes, but the rebukes are meant to teach, to fashion, to incorporate, and what was blacker than coal, it makes whiter than milk.

It is significant that the preceding words are that 'his eyes are more beautiful than
Gen 49:12 wine',* so as to make it clear that charity and the appearance of grace are indicated by 'eyes', just as a loving correction is by 'teeth'. There is good reason for calling them 'more beautiful than wine', for the correction of our chastising God can appear very sharp, because of the fervor of his love, and then the whiteness of the teeth can be appreciated by contrast with the foaming wine, as well. The bite of discipline is not to be judged too severe since it springs from the compassionate eye of grace.

So, then, God has formed and arranged the 'teeth' of his beloved church after the model of his own 'teeth', in so far as she possesses loving zeal, just wrath, gentle indignation, peaceful correction, tranquil rebuke. Consequently, from her state of 'whiteness', it can be clearly seen how great is the interior radiance of her zealous affection. Her teeth bite, therefore, but they do not wound, they eat, but they do not consume. They break without scattering, they sever without tearing, they swallow without swallowing up. Just the contrary: their bite brings health, they strengthen when they eat, they give unity when they break. By dividing they bring together, and by consuming they bring to consummation.

5. Yet those sheep are said to have come up 'from the washing',* and this is appropriate. They would not otherwise be really fit for this work, if there was not full and obvious cleanness in them. Those who, as apostles, have the duty of correcting others, ought to be 'well thought of by outsiders',* and none of them should be in any danger of hearing, 'Physician, heal yourself!'* Nor of hearing, 'Hypocrite, first cast the beam out of your own eye!'* Again, Solomon compares the man 'who sends a message by a foolish messenger',* to a rotten tooth. Besides, the man 'who sends' and the 'messenger' who is sent are one and the same person, a fool in sending, and a fool in being sent. He is 'rotten', as long as he wants to censure other men, though he is unable to teach himself, and he is a fool, as long as he agrees to be a messenger, though he has nothing either new or pleasant to say.

Cf. Sg 4:2

1 Tim 3:7

Lk 4:23

Mt 7:5

Pr 26:6

No, if anyone wants to be 'a washing' as far as I am concerned, he must first 'come

up from the washing', as far as he himself is concerned. If anyone desires to 'shear' me into poverty and patience, so that I may learn from him to become poor and naked and follow the one who 'stood still before his shearer and
Is 53:7 did not open his mouth,'* then he must first practise what he is preaching. If he is to shear without hindrance, then first let him be sheared himself. In the same way, if he is to be a man of zeal, as wise as he is strong, he must show zeal first for himself, and only after that for me. I can believe I am genuinely loved by a man, if I have seen that he shows love for himself. But how can he chew over with me the word of correction or encouragement, if he has a rotten set of teeth? He has himself nothing to eat, and in addition, he has nothing to eat with, so in the end, he dies of hunger.

6. Oh, what toothache the church suffers from nowadays, what great toothache! So many of her teeth are decayed, eaten away by an invisible worm, and they stay on in her mouth, a source of nothing but affliction and misery. Even though they are rotten to the root, they cling stubbornly on, and they resist any attempt to draw them out. Certainly, when it comes to showing zeal for preferment, rank, endowment and wealth, they have nothing less than elephant's tusks, in comparison with the zealousness of the ancient fathers, not to speak of a comparison with the great apostles. But when it comes to zeal for the things of Christ Jesus, and the salvation of the souls for whom Christ died, they seem to become completely impotent

to do any eating.

In short, their teeth are not at all 'like a flock of sheep',* but more like a pack of wolves. *Cf. Sg 6:5* As for the sheep themselves, which they have undertaken to pasture, to wash and to shear, they bite into them with their wolfish teeth, they slaughter them, and they eat them. The unhappy voice of the church cries out against them to the Good Shepherd, 'The sons of men, their teeth are spears and arrows.'* *Ps 57:5* And in answer comes the consoling words of the Holy Spirit, 'God will break their teeth in their mouths.'* *Ps 58:6* He speaks again through Ezekiel: 'I will rescue my flock from their mouths, and they shall be food for them no longer.'* *Ez 34:10* So there is One who will judge these men. As for us, let us leave the wolves and come back to the sheep.

7. But now, here is a problem: why are they called 'sheep'? Would not 'rams' be more appropriate, since theirs is the duty of being zealous on the sheep's behalf, and of protecting them? But the gentleness of these good and loving zealots is better expressed by 'sheep'. It is their duty to live among the sheep as simply one of them, to be in charge of the sheep but purely for the sheep's good and in their company. All the same, the Good Shepherd asks something more from these sheep than from the others. From the others, he is quite content with a single offspring, but from these his demands are more exacting. Hence we find him saying, 'Each one bears twins, not one of them is barren.'* *Sg 6:5*

A double set of young were born to those shepherds of whom we read, 'Watching, and

Lk 2:8 keeping the nightwatch over their flock.'* In fact, for watchmen, there is a twofold duty pertaining to watch-keeping of this type. Scripture says of the first watch-keeping: 'Arise, cry out in the night, at the beginning of the watches; pour out your heart like *Lam 2:19* water.'* And again: 'O God, my God, to *Ps 63:1* you will I watch at break of day.'* But for the second watch-keeping, the flock claims for itself all the duties it involves. For, if by any chance the shepherd of the flock should fall asleep, the wolf may not sleep, but keep awake to slaughter the sheep. He watches late, a reproach to the sleepy and a spur to the slumberer. This is the way in which one of these watchmen stirs up the partner of his watch to a faithful wakefulness. 'Be careful,' he says, 'take care to present yourself as a workman who has no cause to be ashamed, *2 Tim 2:15* rightly handling the word of truth.'* He will certainly avoid any sign of shame, here and now, if he is a workman who works out his own salvation and rightly dispenses 'the word of truth', while at the same time he is careful not to neglect the salvation of others. He has this to say, also, 'Take heed to yourself and to your teaching; hold to that, for by so doing you will save both yourself and those *1 Tim 4:16* who hear you.'*

8. Other ewes, therefore, are pregnant with only a single offspring, because they have a daily supply of milk sufficient for pasturing a single lamb which is their own innocence. Clearly, for this purpose, a double udder is provided for them, almost as though they had within themselves a double merciful-

ness, the loving mercy of which it is written: 'Be kind to your soul, pleasing God.'* First, be kind, and this will make you not displeasing, and then again, be kind, and this will make you pleasing. Be kind to yourself, needy and exiled, to keep you from wasting away in your neediness and being buried in the earth at the last. Be even kinder to your soul so that you can eat the bread of life and come home to the land of your fathers. They are genuinely wicked, genuinely inhuman and outlawed completely from loving mercy, who refuse to be kind to their own individual souls. By their own judgement they condemn themselves, and doom their souls to be consumed by the eternal fires. This is why, in the list of the sevenfold graces of the Spirit, the Spirit of loving kindness comes next to the Spirit of fear. It is this loving kindness that enables every single one of us to learn from the Spirit of fear to be kind to our own soul.*

Sir 30:24

Cf. Sir 30:24

From this double udder then, there comes a double supply of milk, enabling it to keep a fast with respect to the old, and be intent upon the new. It has the milk of self-control, in its detestation of ingrained sinfulness, but the milk of holiness, in its profession of a new way of life. That is why we find both self-control and chastity listed together among the fruits of the Spirit, one indicating the leaving behind of sin, and the other the binding oneself to virtue.

9. Moreover, just as those who are in authority over others need greater holiness, so also do they need deeper loving kindness.

It is necessary for them to have 'breasts better *Cf. Sg 1:1* than wine',* for it is only once that wine is pressed out from the grape, and from the bottle, too, it can only be poured out once. But a great flow does not exhaust the milk in the breasts, it is drawn upon time and again, and does not lessen. This is why they *Sg 6:5* are burdened with 'bearing twins',* in other words, the twofold fruit of love. Theirs is the pre-eminent love that yearns ardently towards God, for its own happiness, and overflows onto its subordinates, seeking the salvation of other men. It is only right that they should be rich with twofold love and reveal breasts swollen with milk, to which these who are to feed from them can have swift recourse.

10. Yes, these fruitful breasts are rivers of milk. This is, in fact, why they deserve the name of 'fruitful breasts', because they are full to the brim with loving fruitfulness, and the more often any mother displays them, the more generously does grace spring up in them, incapable of exhaustion, the more abundantly does it overflow. If any of you is a mother, then, do not be niggardly of your breasts. To be a true mother, you must lay them bare and press them into your children's mouths. Use your breasts to make visible what lies hid within your heart, and let them pour forth the sweet judgement of deepfelt love, tasting of Christ while it nourishes their life.

But as for you, if you are truly to be sons, it must be milk like this, human milk, not the milk of beasts. As the apostle says, 'Seek the *1 Pet 2:2* rational milk which is without guile.'* Then you will not peter out in useless things, nor grow strong in evil things, but, as it says in the same place, 'you will grow up to salvation.'* *1 Pet 2:2*

11. The words that follow: 'Not one of them is barren',* touches indirectly on those mothers who take no care for the sheep, and so are not really mothers at all, because 'they are barren'. For in what sense are they 'mothers', how can they be anything else but 'barren', if they know absolutely nothing of maternal tenderness, care, or love? Although in this present life, they seem to consider themselves among the fruitful mothers, they are cut off from their number, all the same, for they have separated themselves from their goodness! Already, as the Head Shepherd sees it, they do not belong to his sheep because they are not part of them.* On the contrary, they are as far away from them as goats are far removed from sheep.* Why should we wait for the end of time to have the good separated from the bad? No, 'this world is already judged,'* already the sheep have been divided from the goats, one to the right, the other to the left.* *Sg 4:2* *Cf. Jn 10:26* *Cf. Mt 25:32* *Jn 12:31* *Cf. Mt 25:32*

I think it would be fitting, now, to examine how these same words can be applied to the soul that thirsts for God. But the hour is already late, and the small space left of this sermon has no room for this. So I shall make an end of it here, and keep what I have still to say for a new beginning, to the praise and glory of the only Son of God, who with his

Father and the Holy Spirit,
lives and reigns, God,
for ever and ever.
Amen.

SERMON FIFTY-ONE

The beginning of the fifty-first sermon. Of the bride's zealousness, which is symbolized by 'teeth'. Of the abundant humility, which 'flocks of sheep' are meant to represent, and how both these virtues, no less, are indicated by each sheep 'having its twin'.

'YOUR TEETH are a flock of sheep that have come up from the washing; each one has its twin, not one of
Sg 6:5 them is barren.'*

In the commendations that the spouse is bestowing on his beloved, he has been careful to observe a fitting order, so that the very way in which one praise succeeds another is in itself a matter for praise. After praising her hair, a figure of the bride's humility, if only because it takes its origin from former disfigurement of present weakness, he passes on to a eulogy of her teeth where, it seems to me, he is intent on suggesting her zeal for justice. Obviously, he has done well to mention this attribute immediately after the other, since such great humility is the mother of holy zeal.

Consequently, you find this arrangement in the list of beatitudes and virtues in the gospels. When 'the lawgiver gives his blessing'* and blesses those 'who mourn',† that is,

*Cf. Ps 84:6
†Mt 5:4

those who have been brought to tears by compunction for their lack of virtue, he straightaway extends the blessing to those who 'hunger and thirst after justice'.* Clearly, he is setting the degrees and paths of his blessings in a regular series, so that they may go in an orderly progression 'from strength to strength',* moving from the grief of loving devotion to an eagerness for virtue. The apostle continues this same train of thought when he says: 'See what earnestness the godly grief has produced in you, what eagerness to clear yourselves, what indignation, what alarm, what longing, what zeal, what punishment.'* 'Earnestness', 'longing', 'zeal', 'indignation', 'punishment', and the other qualities he enumerated, stressing their connection by putting 'what' between each separate phrase: surely this all seems to have revealed at its sharpest, what we could call 'the zeal' of teeth?

Mt 5:6

Cf. Ps 84:7

2 Cor 7:11

2. So the spouse, praising the zeal of his beloved, and the hunger and thirst with which she craves incessantly to achieve true perfection, says, 'Your teeth are a flock of sheep that have come up from the washing.'* For was it not, in a certain sense, a flock of sheep that Paul counted out for you a little while ago? 'Earnestness', 'eagerness', 'indignation', 'alarm', 'longing', 'zeal', 'punishment'?* A poor little handful of sheep, indeed, if we look at the fewness of their number, but not such a handful if we look at what that number signifies and the fruit of these same sheep.

Sg 6:5

2 Cor 7:11

The number seven rejoices in a sevenfold blessing, if we think of those seven lambs with which Abraham once struck a covenant with Abimelech,* and gave the name of 'Beersheba' to the well he made there, because the number of the lambs was seven.* And now, what of ourselves? If, despite everything, we have the grace to be of the bride's company, we have used these seven lambs of ours which Paul enumerates, to conclude a new treaty with King Abimelech, that is, with the law which tyrannizes over our members.* It is a law that fights against the law of our heart,* as it did to our father Abraham, and tries to lead us away captive to the law of sin. It would make us slaves among the Philistines* and snatch away from us the well of living water.*

Cf. Gen 21:28

**Cf. Gen 21:31—Beersheba is said to mean 'well of seven'.*

Cf. Rom 7:23

Cf. Rom 7:22

Cf. Judg 16:2

Cf. Jn 4:14

In a word, this is the King Abimelech who violently carried Sara off into his house,* and to this very day he has never stopped doing the same thing to us. Within us, there is an incitement to evil, strongly and fearlessly carrying off to its bedchamber, which is the delight that sin gives, the glory of our self-restraint, in other words, 'the woman', which Paul says is 'the glory of the man'.* Ceaselessly and seductively she is urged to give her consent to what will kill her. But God sees to it that our woman returns to us unharmed, for he holds in his hand all the powers of kings and the laws of their kingdoms. And with her, from the house of Abimelech, she bears a thousand silver pieces 'as a veil for her eyes',* that is, to make clear the perfection of her modesty, which, by God's decree, she bore away from so grave, so frequent, so dangerous a combat, out of the hand of Abimelech. As

Cf. Gen 20:3

1 Cor 11:7

Cf. Gen 20:16

a consequence, the very circumstance which seemed likely to threaten the loss of our chastity, has in a wonderful way served only to make its crown more resplendent.

We can go even further, and say, that not only is there a greater crown for the one who has been protected, but she is also more careful to be protected. From the frequency with which our eyes are wounded, we learn to seal a treaty with our eyes, to let nothing indecent even cross our minds. This is why, after she had been given and had accepted 'a veil for her eyes',* obviously intended as a trusty shield for her modesty, scripture goes on to say that wherever Sara went, it would remind her that she had been snatched away.* So that, in time to come, the abductor's contamination, though so short-lived, would have a perpetual place in her memory as something very blameworthy. She was caught once by the tempter, and her veiled face and what we might call the public emblem of her purity, betokens this.

Cf. Gen 20:16

Cf. Gen 20:2

3. However, all I have said is merely by way of illustrating the bride's zeal in relation to modesty. Her zeal flourishes with no less vigor in the exercise of other virtues as well. Her teeth are always eager to be eating, and whatever they come across, they eat, until in the end they become accustomed to choicer fare, and then what is common and sour and less choice disgusts them. Certainly, the bride feels sickened by all worldly anxieties, and she thinks everything common and sour if it does not taste to her of the savor of heaven or her beloved's charity. For

Cf. 1 Cor 12:31 she is zealous for the better gifts,* especially for the best and most precious gift of all,
Cf. 1 Cor 13:13 which is charity.* This is what she eats, this is what she hungers for every hour. She hungers for it even while she eats it, and when she has
Cf. Sir 24:29 eaten, her hunger is still with her.*

In her hunger, she has many powerful incentives to her desire, so that the richer the table that is spread for her, the sharper is her tooth and the stronger her zeal for good. For indeed, her hunger has an edge to it. In the first place, there is the hunger she remembers having felt when she toiled in a
Cf. Lk 15:13 distant land.* She recalls many weighty things
Cf. Lk 7:47 which were forgiven her,* and she longs very
Cf. 1 Jn 4:19 greatly to love him who first loved her.* Even though, to her beloved's eyes, his own beauty has been graciously bestowed on her, still,
Cf. Sg 4:9 how this beauty 'wounds his heart',* how it enters into the very depths of his being! Or, more truly, how it leads the very depth
Cf. Eph 4:8 of all her being 'captive into captivity'.*

All this, then, gives the bride very strong reason to be zealous, and she finds no respite from her zeal short of the full vision of her beloved. Then, too, she finally looks at those souls whom, from all she has read or heard about them, she knows have devoted themselves entirely to nothing but love. Their passionate eagerness provides her, as it were, with the sharpest of spurs, ever present beside her, immovably fixed. As often as she sees before her such examples of the blessed practice of virtue, their incentive sets her on fire, she is stimulated by their spur, and in holy rivalry, hastens away with them, eager to
Cf. Phil 3:12 run, if only, somehow or other, she may attain.*

4. Yet that zeal is full of meekness, that hunger is rich in the spirit of obedience. The bride knows nothing of the jealousy of the jealous,* and she never journeys in the company of sickly envy.* The path she has chosen for herself, the only path, is the path of charity. So she aims straight at her destination and hastens towards it, but without contention. She puts forth every effort to run vigorously, but without presuming that she will be able to outrun everybody also. She tries not to be found below the expected standard, although she would blush to show herself as above it. Accordingly, after the example of her master, her eagerness for the greatest leads her to embrace the least. It is because she yearns for one of the highest places at the wedding feast that she is so careful to take the lowest.* The result is that her spouse takes equal joy in a zeal so humble and a humility so zealous that neither virtue impedes the other but rather gives it life and fire. 'Your teeth', he says, 'are a flock of sheep,'* precisely because being zealous for noble things makes her aware of her own ignobility, and she feels herself one of the lowly, though she runs with the swift.*

Cf. Ps 37:1

Cf. Wis 6:25

Cf. Lk 14:10

Sg 6:5

Cf. Rom 12:16

Yet, despite her zeal for justice, her zeal for humility, as well as her zeal for gentleness, she does not consider herself as having attained justice except in knowing clearly that she is lowly and unassuming. For she knows who it was who said, 'Thus we ought to fulfill all justice',* openly preaching to John the gospel of humility. And indeed, he showed the greatness of humility in a very marked way

Mt 3:15

by calling it 'all justice'.

To safeguard humility and gentleness, the bride has the constant recollection of her *Cf. Ex 14:30* departure from Egypt,* a recollection that resembles the whiteness of one fresh from washing. She is anxious to avoid the ingratitude characteristic of the Jews, in case she should hear, as they did: 'They did not keep in mind his power, on the day when he *Ps 78:43* redeemed them from the power of the foe'.* So, like somebody fresh from a bath, as if she *Sg 6:5* had today 'come up from the washing',* she is gentle to everybody and strives to be more humble than others in all she does. Further, she is careful to conform humbly to the rest of the flock, not wanting to stand out as exceptional but to unite with the flock as one like the rest of them. Hence the express word- Ibid. ing: 'Your teeth are a flock of sheep,'* promising nothing higher than the flock or outside it, but keeping within the flock and with it.

5. It does not seem to me without significance that the words used here are not 'shorn sheep', but simply 'sheep'. It makes it very clear that they are washed, but yet shorn, having, in fact, newly 'come up from the Ibid. washing'.* We know, moreover, that sheep that have just been washed, have a keener appetite for eating, since their fleece has put on a new cleanliness from its bath, and is ready for the shearer's hand. Consequently, the same is true of the soul that loves Jesus, and she is very zealous for humility. She does not presume to count herself among the shorn sheep, that is, those souls that have

thrown away all worldly anxieties and every solicitude for their own flesh.

She remembers, of course, that a burden has been laid upon her. To be in charge of others means inescapable anxiety, which is why, earlier in the song, she says, 'they made me keeper of the vineyards, my own vineyard I did not keep.'* Indeed, very often she has gone down to the washing, to cleanse her fleece. She needs to wash away the dust of the earth's grime, which inevitably sullies her, wherever she feeds or sleeps, and hence her tireless return to 'the washing'. Moreover, coming up from the washing often whets her teeth to 'hunger and thirst after justice'.* She has become humbler, gentler, more prudent, more reverent, more fervent in charity for her brothers and love for her spouse. The spouse means to express zeal for all these virtues when he speaks of his bride's 'teeth', and they are marvelously resharpened by her constant frequentation of the 'washing' and the restoration to whiteness of her fleece.

Sg 1:5

Mt 5:6

6. And you, too, my brothers, do you not learn from daily experience? I see, and with great joy, how you rival one another in going up to the 'sea of brass',* that stands before the gates of the tabernacle, and I see you in turn coming back to feed there all the more eagerly for having so recently been washed. Without delay, you hasten back to the altar of holocaust, and there, ceremonially and in a contrite spirit, you sacrifice your whole selves to the Lord your God. Then borne on by the fervor of holy devotion, you make your reverent approach to the very holy of holies.

1 Chron 18:8

You go forward with confidence to that very great and lofty tabernacle, 'where Christ is,
Col 3:1 seated at God's right hand,'* there to burn, at the altar of incense, the fragrant incense of earnest prayer. That prayer, 'like a perfumed
Sg 3:6 column of smoke,'* will take a smooth path to the ears of the Lord Jesus. For he is the true high priest, and it is he who lays in your thuribles coals from his own altar and incense from his own country. It is he who draws out that vapor of scented smoke, he who directs the passage of the incense, so that no harm
Cf. Rev 8:4 befall it on the way.* It is he, by the hand of his holy angel, who receives what is offered
Cf. Ez 20:41 and makes it 'an odor of sweetness'.*

Believe me, my brothers, from now on that odor will never disappear, that smoke will never cease, that sweetness will never die away. Your prayer has been inscribed in the
Cf. Rev 3:5 book of life,* and can never be blotted out. That living odor has been taken up into the
Cf. Jn 14:6 Life,* and now can escape from the tyranny of death; that sweetness, drawn up into God's own nostrils, has now passed beyond any fear of danger. Moreover, there is an angel there, well able to keep safe for you the prayerful incense you have entrusted to him, enclosed in a golden thurible of the most selfless charity and placed in his hands. He will only give it up on that day when the books are opened to the view and the incense of the thuribles is shown for what it is.

7. And now, my brothers, consecrated to both these altars, take your place before them. But, if you are to come forward in purity, and be called God's priests in truth,

and go around the Lord's altar with a clean heart,* then, I beg of you, do not be slow to wash your hands.* When you have clean hands, your prayer springs forth with greater purity and freedom. Its passage is swifter, it penetrates more deeply, it enters God's presence more pleasingly. So it should not grieve you, far less embarrass you, to be immersed often in this cleansing water. To go down to the washing is, then, a small thing, but to come up from it works great things for the soul. The apostle calls it 'the washing of regeneration and renewal of the Holy Spirit'.* Yes, at each single washing there is a renewal of the noble image of God, with which we have been sealed and signed. When the dust of the former creature is purged away, the new creature that is within us is formed anew,* from 'day to day',† that is, 'from one new beginning to another'.*

Cf. Ps 26:6
Ibid.
Cf. Tit 3:5
**Cf. 2 Cor 5:17*
†Ps 19:2
**Rom 12:2*

8. So this repeated washing has two effects: the cleanliness of all our righteousness, which we could describe as our 'fleece', is restored by the humility of that descent, and our very zeal for virtue puts on fresh eagerness, as if our teeth had been newly sharpened. I think that this twofold effect is the twin offspring which the verse immediately refers to: 'Each one has its twin, not one of them is barren.'* It is not just that the effect is twofold, but that it is twin. One womb brought them simultaneously to birth, that one birth simultaneously cleansed them. At one and the same time, there was a beginning and a completion for purity and righteousness, for innocence and holiness, for

Sg 6:5

the renewal of virtue and the zeal for virtue, for purity of conscience and a hunger for goodness. Without any doubt, there is a close connection between the purity with which you come up out of the waters, and the alacrity with which you hasten to the pastures of life, as well as the eagerness with which you stay there in those pastures.

9. Consequently, I want that 'washing' to be seen now as meaning more than our practice of confessing our sins to each other. It means also the daily practice of confessing them, with heartfelt sorrow, to our high priest, God. Or rather, it is neither one nor the other, but a washing of tender love. Since the way to God lies open to us, we are allowed to rinse, in the fountain of his loving kindness, the fleeces of our poor righteousness, which we seem to bear about with us.

Indeed, for the bride too, it appears to me that this is the 'washing' with which she habitually and often washes her sheep, in other words, her gentle and humble sentiments. And there is Mary Magdalen, who was taken from the chariots of Pharaoh, but whom our Solomon compared to one of his
Cf. Sg 1:9 horsemen,* and, over and above, bestowed
Sg 1:2 on her the 'kiss of his mouth'* in that he made her grow in grace. He even placed on her head his royal diadem, and raised her to the glory of being his bride. Now it is this very woman whom I hear of as having been totally washed clean, totally purified, in those most lovely waters. It was this washing that made it possible for her beloved to say on her behalf, 'Many sins are forgiven her, because she has

loved much.'* *Lk 7:47*

You can see how terse a summary of perfection we have here, precisely because the water of this washing is living water, with life in it to purify us more than any other water can. Its power to form us into a new creature, is greater and more speedy, as it were, water flowing from heaven. So, in the privacy of her bridal chamber, the bride is accustomed to this familiar washing so as to cleanse herself and make herself whiter than snow.* *Cf. Ps 51:7* She uses it to make her teeth look like the teeth of her spouse, 'whiter than milk',* *Gen 49:12* so that, by regaining their whiteness, they may catch the sharp edge of an eager zeal. She takes the greatest care that they are always found so hungry for charity that they never find themselves having as much of it to eat as they would like. The virtue of fervent love has the quality of persevering in good works, and yet is always desiring something better. It forgets what is past, as though it were of little importance, and strives towards greater things.

It is very fitting, them that love like this should be compared to both teeth and sheep, seeing that, as already mentioned, it burns with the keenness of zeal and is gentle with the tenderness of humility. And likewise, these two fruits of righteousness can aptly be described as born twin-lambs but they are assigned to the sheep since the power of emulation to glow or to persevere comes, in both instances, from humility. Consider well, I beg you, how great a virtue humility is. The Holy Spirit makes it fruitful, and it is heavy with 'twin offspring'. It is zealous for 'the highest of all gifts',* and yet the higher it becomes, the lowlier it strives to be.

1 Cor 13:13

10. Moreover, the words that follow: 'Not one of them is barren',* underline the fervency of zeal, which admits of no carelessness, no idleness, absolutely no sterility. This sentence comes as a piercing blow to our indolence. We are sluggards, wrapt in a false security, withering away in a barrenness that helps no one. The stock we come from is noble,* for our ancestors were shepherds of the sheep, and they were rich in flocks. But we have a poor little handful of sheep, and for the most part, they are barren. In fact, we are sons unworthy of their birth, refusing to labor over the increase of our sheep, and in consequence they die all too often from disease and starvation and the savage onslaughts of bloodthirsty wolves.

Sg 6:5

Cf. Tob 5:19

But I proclaim, brothers, that our profession is humility.* Everything that has to do with our outward behavior, the habit we show to the world, the mutual encounter whenever brother meets brother, the mutual reverence when brothers sit down together, the readiness to obey, and all the other marks of humility which our forebears recommended to us these could be called 'flocks of sheep', no small flocks. But there must be a desire for inward humility, that humility of heart that the only Lamb of God taught us when he said, 'Learn of me, for I am meek and humble of heart,'* so that all the humble behavior we profess is voluntary, coming forth from the pasture of a fruitful heart. If this desire does

**Cf. Bernard, Ep. 132.1; SBOp 7:328-9.*

Mt 11:29

not fatten our flocks, we shall have scrawny sheep, barren and diseased, and they will be a powerful reproach to their shepherds' lack of interest.

11. Yes, but the bride is zealous and careful about these things. She watches anxiously over her flock, in case the spouse should one day come when she is sleeping, and find some barrenness there. And so, she deserves his blessing, because he finds her watching,* and *Cf. Lk 12:37*
he crowns her with twin offspring, because she shuns the idleness of sterility. So she is rich with the fruit of charity as well as humility, and with this twofold offspring, she deserves to give eternal pleasure to her spouse, the Son of the Father, who with his Father and the Holy Spirit, lives and reigns, God, for ever and ever. Amen.

SERMON FIFTY-TWO

The beginning of the fifty-second sermon. How this description fits the church, whose 'cheeks' are chaste souls. When the church was being persecuted they fought for their chastity and became 'a broken pomegranate', that is, a distinguished portion of that glorious band of united witnesses. But when the church is at peace, struggling against unchaste desires and an enemy she cannot see, then these souls cover her with the veil of holy shame and admonition, as with the pomegranate rind, which, like the seeds hidden within it, conceals even her characteristic virtues.

'LIKE THE RIND of a pomegranate, so are your cheeks, concealing your
Sg 6:6 secrets.'*

We find these same words said by the spouse in his earlier list of his bride's graces, though a few of them are different. There he said, 'Like a broken pomegranate, so are your
Sg 4:3 cheeks, concealing what lies within.'* But here, instead of a broken pomegranate, he speaks of its rind, and instead of 'what lies within', he refers to 'secrets'. Moreover, round about the beginning of this marriage song, I find the bride's cheeks singled out for praise and being said to be 'beautiful as a
Cf. Sg 1:9 turtle dove's.'* At any rate, these different

ways of praising show a great richness of praise. Since not a leaf falls from a tree without our Father's will,* still less would it be possible for any leaf to drop idly from this tree, the most towering and fruitful of all the trees of the forest. Indeed, it would be easier for heaven and earth to pass away than for even one word among the words of the Word, the Wisdom of God the Father. Rather, not one iota, not one dot, or any of his words can be spoken of as 'passing away'.*

Cf. Mt 10:29

Cf. Mt 5:18

2. In consequence, by 'the cheeks' of the church (for these words ought first to be applied to her, by the generosity of her spouse), I think we have a symbol of chaste souls. They are compared to the 'cheeks of a turtle dove',* because it is they in particular who hear 'the voice of the turtle dove in our land'.* It is they who have chosen to follow the Lamb of God, the virgin's Son, wherever he goes,* taking a way that is all flowers. Yes, the 'voice of the turtle dove' is the voice of the Lord Jesus, who set a holy seal on the glory of purity by his virginal conception. His was the voice they heard, with ears blessed by him, who with the promise of a glorious reward, called them to the high state and prize of chastity. In the full flower of their early youth, as if at the very beginning of spring, they waited with open ears for 'the voice of the turtle dove'. But to all the voices that bring death, they shut their ears, and they clung only to the pure embrace of him of whom it is written: 'The body is not meant for fornication, but for the Lord, and the Lord is meant for the body.'*

Sg 4:3

Sg 2:12

Rv 14:4

1 Cor 6:13

The old, familiar ways of the world were not for them. They turned deliberately aside, and by a bond that nothing can untie, they consecrated their souls and bodies to that most beautiful dove, Christ, and as it were, entered into a sacred marriage relationship with him. Mindful of their secret and of the contract they have entered into with their heavenly spouse, they avoid all public places and resolve to live in solitude, being above all things wary of anything that could endanger their innocence. They groan with a most chaste compunction, and they renounce the consolations of all things under heaven, having as their sole desire to please him to whom they have offered themselves. But for long periods, they are not able to enjoy at will the presence of their mate, that is, of their heavenly spouse. All too often, indeed, he flies away to his heavenly solitude.

It is when he flies away that the turtle dove mourns and grieves, lamenting her widowhood and mourning the loneliness of her solitude. From then on, she turns in disgust from all that is green and growing, regarding it as poison and disdaining all consolation. She makes it clear that she is true to her marriage vow, and that nothing, even though she is widowed, can make her break it. She is utterly convinced that it is better to fade away for the sake of him to whom she has vowed herself, and she prefers to lament over him who is absent rather than rejoice over the world which is present.

This, then, is the way a soul of this kind loves, this is the way she sighs, this is the way

she turns from all the blossoms of life on earth, happy in her solitude and pining away over the memory of her spouse. She is an exile here below, but her spouse comes to visit her. He comes to see his lovely bride, he comforts her in her desolation and praises her, all distressed as she is. And it is fitting, very fitting, that he should say to her, 'Your cheeks are as beautiful as a turtle dove's.'* *Sg 1:9*
Like the cheeks of that turtle to whom you have bound yourself, so are your cheeks, cheeks of beauty. By loving me, by sighing for me, by imitating me, the charm of your cheeks has now clothed itself in the beauty of my cheeks. Even if they are not yet wholly like mind, nevertheless, the bond of union, has already made them to some extent alike.

I have said all this about the first compliment that is paid the bride's cheeks, but, to the edification of us all, it has already been elucidated, much more fully and in a way much more worthy of praise, by the eminent writer who undertook the commentary on the first part of the poem.* **Bernard, SC 40; SBOp 2:24-8; CF 7:199-209.*

3. Further on in the poem, the bride's cheeks are compared to broken pieces of pomegranate,* implying that the chastity of the church's virgins has reached a still higher stage. In loyalty to her virginity, the church has been publicly put to the test by countless different forms of terrifying cruelty, beyond the limits of human strength and almost beyond the limits of belief. She has been tempted by blandishments and anguished by tortures. To make the triumph of holiness more wonderful, as a spectacle to God, to the *Cf. Sg 4:3*

Cf. 1 Cor 4:9 angels and to men,* the weaker sex has advanced into this field of battle. But near at hand, implanted in the heart of those who love him, is he who says, 'I am the flower of
Sg 2:1 the field, the lily of the valleys',* in other words, the strength of those who struggle, the beauty of those who fight, the crown of those who conquer. Those in whom the flesh has withered away, but in whom the modesty of the flesh has burst into beautiful flower, have ended their lives triumphantly, bearing away, like the prize of battle, the 'flower of the field'.

This assembly, then, of pure hearts, in the earthen vessels of womanly fragility, what else can we call it but 'a broken pomegranate', a distinguished portion, as it were, of that great army of martyrs? The glorious union of the martyrs I think could well be compared to a pomegranate. For love of the christian faith, they fought as one, united in devotion even unto death. Despite the many thousands who fought against them and the agonies of carefully devised tortures, a great and wholly indescribable miracle of divine strength kept them from faltering in their faith, even for a moment. Rather, they came out of their tortures even stronger than before. In fact, even in the outward show of their body, they have the true pomegranate color, resplendent with their sacred blood, but within, the martyr is ruddy with a most ardently burning charity. And yet, all the same, the martyr is radiant white within, and to the eyes that judge by the interior, as the ruddy hue speaks with full confidence of fervent love, so does the white speak of the most joyful hope of eternal blessedness.

4. Yes, this pomegranate is the special fruit of that great tree that never sheds its leaves, that will bear its fruit openly at its own time,* that the bride is speaking of when she says: 'As the apple tree among the trees of the wood, so is my beloved among the young men.'* Of course, all God's chosen ones are fruits of this tree, but, as we have said before, the martyrs unite with such impenetrable courage, that, as if they were a pomegranate, they claim for themselves the highest place in this tree. Clearly, the 'broken pieces of this pomegranate' are a pre-eminent and illustrious part of the church, being those chaste souls who thought that to fall in death in defense of their purity was a mighty foretaste, even now, of the glory that is to come.* So it is a 'broken pomegranate', broken by so many sufferings, split in half by such various types of torture, torn to pieces by such bitter pains, broken indeed in the body, and yet ever remaining wholly unbroken in the spirit.* It grows into an ever greater wholeness of faith and charity, in the way that an earthenware pot though weaker than other vessels requires a fierce blow to be broken.

Cf. Ps 1:3

Sg 2:3

**Cf. Cyprian,* De habitu virginum *3; PL 4:443B*

**Cf. Novatian (=Ps Cyprian),* De disciplina et bono pudicitiae *7; PL 4:823A.*

5. But when the Sun of justice looks down from on high, that winter of stormy weather is forgotten. Gentle spring weather takes its place, and the voice of the turtle dove, heard long ago by those turtle doves who so bravely strove for their chastity, begins once more to be heard in our land, also.* This voice, too, seems to be speaking gently and

Cf. Sg 2:12

tranquilly about the holiness of purity, for now the mad rage of persecution has died away and the right time is at last come to
Cf. 1 Kgs 5:4 build the temple,* free from the evil adver-
1 Kgs 5:4 sary and the throng of malignants.*
1 Cor 3:17 To be sure, 'the temple of God is holy',* and the whole church is a church of saints, whether living in marriage or widowhood or in virginal chastity. Yet the secret heart of this temple, what we might call its 'holy of holies', is the continence of those who are not involved in the bonds of wedlock but follow the sublimer paths of chastity. All of these hear the voice of the turtle dove, because they have learned from the Holy Spirit to lament the enticing motions of itching lust. They have beautiful cheeks, 'like the turtle's', feeling ashamed before disgraceful things, and blushing at having even thought of what is disgraceful. In fact, so chaste and modest are their cheeks, that they protect their chastity with modesty, and with a godly veil of confession, just as if it were the rind of a pomegranate, they make haste to cover up the secrets of their beauty. Should I say 'cover up' or 'reveal'? Better to say both at once, since to reveal humbly is, in fact, to have wisely 'covered up'.

6. So, in these words, the spouse is praising the chastity of his bride, the church. When her heavenly spouse gives the church peace from heaven, she is careful to preserve her chastity, for it is in no less danger when there is no sword to fear and she is caressed by tranquil peace, than when, as in the past, the persecutor was at her heels and the palm of

victory smiled on the threshold. Now especially, her bitterness is at its most bitter in time of peace,* when pestilential frenzy rushes more cruelly than any weapon of riotous living. Wherever she turns her eyes, it is not in her power to avoid the sight of this woman, all flattery and persistence, whose words are smoother than oil.* It is a case of 'fighting without, and fear within,'* because exteriorly the temptress lures us by her example, and in order to attack us, she is in constant touch with her invisible enemy which sleeps within our bosom,* namely, our fleshly appetites.

Cf. Is 38:17

Cf. Pr 5:3

2 Cor 7:5

Cf. Mic 7:5

The sword of iron, then, has ceased,* but a sword of fire now threatens us, much more penetrating and far more terrible. Consequently, for every single bride who is battling for her chastity, the refuge is to be very careful in studiously cloaking herself beneath the covering of godly modesty and to have a sort of bashfulness veiling her before the eyes of her spouse. The very 'rind' of her careful modesty, and a modesty coming from her blushes and the sense of shame within her, makes her pleasing to him. Then she will confidently raise her face to him and say: 'I have taken pleasure in your truth.'* It is because of that truth that 'my shame is always before me,'* and 'I have made known to you my sin'.* Moreover, modesty can be found in two different ways. Either she avoids the movements of temptation before they begin, preventing them, with her maternal authority, from even raising their head, or else, if these passions are already in full

Cf. 1 Mac 9:73

Ps 26:3

Ps 44:16

Ps 32:5

career, she reproves, whips, and subdues them, with what we could call a severe freedom. This modesty is of a very great excellence and it leads to a high degree of glory. It preserves the safety of what is still untarnished, and what has been tarnished, it renews. Besides this, humility and prudence, godliness and charity, in fact, all the virtues, receive from it a great increase of grace and are made ready for a considerable amount of glory. So it fortifies and encompasses, as it were, within one rind, all her gifts of virtue, like the pleasing inner parts of the pomegranate, and it conceals them from the gaze of men and from any eye but God's. Obviously, this 'rind' of modesty is a good one, for it conceals all that is good in case it be seen by anyone except God alone, and even more does it conceal what is bad so that it cannot be seen at all, even by God.

7. It is well said therefore, 'as the rind of the pomegranate, so are your cheeks apart
Sg 6:6 from your secrets';* for evidently this shining modesty sets any timid and modest soul apart from its secrets, hiding her good deeds under a cloak of bashfulness, and burying her faults in a secret hiding place through shamefacedness, fear and confession. When both these things are kept hidden, she herself becomes in a wonderful way set apart from her secrets, while at the same time, these secret things remain her own, the good actions destined to earn the glory of happiness the faults as secret spurs to the guarding of her holiness.

8. Or, perhaps, he says: 'concealing se-
Ibid. crets',* gently hinting rather than explicitly

stating, so as to mean more by saying less. Mysteriously commending her secrets, he points to the hidden undercurrent of groaning for the preservation, growth and renewal of any virtue, but particularly charity. Everything on the surface, which encompasses the exterior man, for example, in vigils, labors, fasts, disciplines and all the other exercises of this holy warfare, which are merely on the outside, are, in comparison, like the pomegranate skin when put beside what lies hid within. Speaking to God, who sees into all secrets, one of the saints says of the souls like these: 'My groans are not hidden from you.'* He says, too: 'My mouth was not secret to you, when I was being fashioned by you in secret.'*

Ps 38:9

Ps 139:14

So, what is exterior, like the pomegranate rind, has a pleasant pomegranate color, but it is what lies hid interiorly that gives the refreshment. The external pleases men, the internal is what God looks for, what the angels find lovable, what gives the soul itself grace. The external is certainly a strong retaining wall to keep us safe, a control that supports our chastity, a reinforcement for our self-restraint. But he who searches the heart and loins,* who sees what is invisible, who passes judgement on what is secret, sees; in this case, he pronounces judgement on the hidden things of his bride. True enough, he passes judgement on them, but the judgement is in their favor. Even if he keeps the secrets of other men for the last day and its revelations, so that 'every man then will have his praise from God,'* that is tedious for the bride, or

Cf. Ps 7:10

1 Cor 4:5

rather, it is too long for the spouse to wait such a time for his bride's praise. He is a magnificent praiser, and so he praises her. With utter kindness and love, he praises what is beautiful externally and what is charming internally, what has been achieved for all to see, whether for her own salvation or that of others, and what has been done in private, for her own happiness and the glory of her spouse.

9. Now would be the time to apply these words to the bride of the Word, namely, to any soul who clings with all her heart to the Lord Jesus, but the length of this sermon could not possibly contain it. To leave space for this, it will have to be cut short. At the same time, I must call upon the Lord, our strength and our praise, asking that he may begin what we would say in his honor, begin it, carry it through and end it, for he is the giver, the helper, the rewarder, our direction, courage and recompense, Jesus Christ, the Father's only Son, who with the same Father and the Holy Spirit, lives and reigns, God, for ever and ever. Amen.

SERMON FIFTY-THREE

The beginning of the fifty-third sermon. That 'the bride's cheeks' symbolize her reserve and patience, which are compared by the spouse to 'the rind of a pomegranate', that is, to his own reserve and patience; and that earlier, the patience of the bride was said to be 'a broken piece' of this pomegranate, because the bride shares, through grace in what the spouse possesses fully and completely.

'LIKE THE RIND of a pomegranate, so are your cheeks, concealing your secrets.'* *Sg 6:6*

I have not forgotten that in the last sermon I bound myself to give you another sermon in honor of some one soul that loves Jesus and embraces him with complete and entire devotion. Any soul that is aware within itself of so great a grace, does not lightly lay claim to the title of bride. The right to it will come from the answer of the Holy Spirit and from the judgement of a clean conscience. But for the most part, with regard to these magnificent eulogies of the spouse, anyone who is like me will stand with drooping pinions, bemoaning his inability to feel that praise of this kind applies to him. But at the same time, there is joy in even understanding that this should be a cause of grief and to have deserved, at least on the score of grieving, some little companionship with bride and bridegroom. Such a man, even though the spouse may not as yet speak to him, can nevertheless be glad for the one who has deserved to hear the spouse speaking; he can share the bride's joy.

Jn 3:29 Of course, 'he who has the bride, is the spouse',* and she who has the spouse, is the bride. She 'has' him, in that she clings to the spouse as his bride, she holds him as a spouse there before her and speaks to him there before her and embraces him there before her, and when he is not there, she yearns for him. The spouse has acted graciously to me, if I have been privileged, all unworthy as I am, to be one of those cognizant of, or witness to, the loving conversation he sweetly holds with his bride about their love for each other. Perhaps, as those flaming javelins dart between them, some tiny spark of love may fly from them to my heart, and then, even if I am not all on fire as I should wish, at least I will not perish of the icy cold I feel at present. I may not deserve to be taken deep into the spouse's heart with his bride, but at least it will not be my lot to be 'vomited out' with the tepid.* *Cf. Rev 3:16*

But I must not keep you waiting any longer. Listen then, and, unless you have meanwhile come up with something better, tell me what you think of what I have understood these words of the spouse to mean. In my opinion, the 'cheeks' of the bride designate her reserve and patience. Obviously, I am influenced here by what happened to the spouse's cheeks, knowing that he gave his cheeks to them that 'plucked' them.* Clearly, on this occasion, when he most graciously revealed his sacred cheeks, his reserve was most disgracefully abused, and his patience put to the test. But our Lord, the true Samson, not with the cheek-bone of an ass, but with his own (or rather, with a cheek that, because it was his own, was truly asinine'*), struck down thousands of the people who surrounded him.† They all wounded him without any reason,* but he had a reason, his love, a reason known only to himself and his eternal Father, and he wounded them, not by returning on their cheek the wound they had given, but by offering them his other cheek,* too. Yes, he showed them both his cheeks, namely, the cheek of reserve, to receive insult, as well as the cheek of patience, to receive blows.

Cf. Is 50:6

**An untranslatable pun on* asinus, *a precious stone.*

†Cf. Judg 15:16
**Cf. Jn 18:23*

Cf. Lk 18:32

Hence we read that he was spat upon, that there was spittle on his cheeks and they were struck,* so that reproaches might show the full extent of his modesty, while blows revealed how much he suffered. Thus he was to be both put to shame and distressed. It follows that this very 'plucking of his cheeks', of which scripture most truly says: 'I gave my cheeks to them that plucked them,'* contains equally insult and anguish, though the gospel account passes this over in silence. Moreover, perverted wickedness shows its cunning in bringing about this kind of death. 'Let us', said wickedness, 'condemn him to a disgraceful death'.* 'Let us,' said wickedness again, 'put wood upon his bread.'* In other words, according to what it says in the law, let him

Cf. Mt 26:67

Is 50:6

Wis 2:20

Jer 11:9

be considered accursed, let him be repudiated by everyone, since he will be seen
Cf. Deut 21:23 hanging from a tree.* And so for all time, Jesus crucified will be 'a stumbling block to
1 Cor 1:23 Jews, and folly to the gentiles.'*

2. But the Lord Jesus accepted death gladly. Not only did he let it rack his whole body with pain, but he also let it open out his whole soul to public shame. It was as if he was offering both his cheeks, thinking nothing at all, as the apostle says, of the shame, con-
Cf. Heb 12:2 tempt and grief.* The Word, who is the Wisdom of God the Father, knew very well what this kind of passion would have as its reward, what a sacrament it would be, what salvation it would bring. There is no doubt that it was the ignominy of the crucified that restored what was lost through our ignominy, and whatever in the way of grief or joy sin had besmeared, the grief of the cross blotted it out. In short, the putting to shame of such awe-inspiring greatness is our redemption from being put to shame eternally, and at the same time, his suffering is our remedy against having to suffer for ever.

3. Seeing that Christ wished, in his usual manner, to compare the bride's cheeks to these cheeks of his, I do not think that even he could find another simile that would praise her more highly. Here there does not seem to be anything that might be considered as below the standard of whole-hearted commendation. And so he says, 'Like the rind of a
Sg 6:6 pomegranate, so are your cheeks,'* intending that the pomegranate should be taken as meaning himself, and the rind of the

pomegranate that very humble cloak of patience with which the king of glory shrouded himself so as to intercept either of the attacks of his furious enemies, which we described above. For this cloak served him as an armor that nothing could pierce. It was like a most impregnable rind, hiding from the eyes, as it were, of both visible and invisible enemies, the glory of the divinity that lay concealed within. On the rind, indeed, they could vent their fury, but they could not lay a finger on what was interiorly hidden.

The pomegranate we are speaking of is plainly a fruit of the tree of life, a satisfying and blissful refreshment for all who are in the paradise of my God. This is why it stands in the middle of paradise,* so as to be at hand for everyone who stretches out a hand to it. In this fruit there is complete redemption of the forbidden fruit that was seized unrightfully. The taste of one takes away the guilt of eating the other; to bite the broken pieces of the one brings life, and with wonderful speed heals the death that comes from biting the other.*

Cf. Gen 2:9

Cf. Gen 2:17

4. It is for this reason, in fact, that it says earlier in the poem: 'Like the broken pieces of a pomegranate, so are your cheeks.'* The spouse intended 'broken pieces' to be understood as meaning a sharing in his great gentleness and patience. Solely by participating in that, as if by eating the broken pieces, every virtuous soul becomes gentle and patient. Otherwise, should any of these souls dare to take anything to themselves from another quarter, and not from the cheeks of Jesus and

Sg 4:3

with the taste of pomegranate, they would
Cf. Jer 17:8 have to fear what will happen when hot
Cf. Jer 17:8 weather comes.* When the sun is fierce,
and beats down upon them, they will know a
parching thirst. But anyone who is a man of
might, prepared beforehand for the combat,
bites into this pomegranate. In its broken
pieces he will find refreshment when burning
anguish is upon him and when he is parched
by fevers of soul or body. Yes, if anyone is
thirsty, let him come to the cheeks of Jesus,
Cf. Jn 7:37 and there he will find a living fountain.* To
this very day, as scripture tells us, that foun-
tain is known as 'the fountain of him who
Jdg 15:19 calls it from the cheek.'* You know the
story, no need to tell it all again.

5. But there is a great and wondering delight to see the fulfillment in the cheek-bone of our Samson of what was symbolized long ago in the cheek-bone of an ass and the first Samson. For our sake, our Samson knew the burning heat of weariness and shame and sorrow, during his passion. From no other source than from the zeal of his own holiness (what we might call 'the molar teeth of his cheek'), he drew forth a fountain of living water in which to find refreshment. Having driven away his earlier thirst and dryness, he cast off all fear, distress and sorrow, and girding himself, as if with a sword with the spirit of freedom that is natural to him, he cried aloud, speaking in a spirit of peace, joy
and confidence, 'The cup that my Father has
Jn 18:11 given me, shall I not drink it?'*

So he drank, completely, joyfully and willingly, the cup held out by his Father. He drank from the water of living refreshment which he himself, as we have said, caused to spring up out of his own suffering, and gave him the delight of total joy. Anyone who drinks from this fountain is a martyr, is a Samson, is impregnable to all assault. It follows that to this very day, this fountain is called 'the fountain of him who calls it from the cheek,'* because anyone at all, who calls on the name of the Lord 'from Jesus' cheek', meaning that he looks to him alone for patience, since he is truly the patience of all who are patient, will draw water from that fountain. Then in another sense it will become 'the fountain of the man who calls it from the cheek', because the water that he has drunk will become 'a fountain within him of living water, springing up to eternal life.'*

Jdg 15:19

Jn 14:4

6. 'O Lord God of my salvation,'* how tempestuous are these clouds in which you have enwrapped yourself! You surrender yourself, you reveal yourself, you expose yourself to everything these godless murderers, who know no shame, decided to do to you. You are a sun serenely shining, but you hide this from the eyes of the godless by the dense cloud of your affliction and ignominy, and still more by the cloud of your interior patience. So you have covered the sun with a cloud, as once, long ago, it was prophesied of you.* You have clothed the heavens with darkness,* and you have hidden omnipotence under weakness and wisdom under simplicity. You have made freedom look like trembling submission, gladness look like distress, contentment look like suffering, and you have

Ps 38:22

Cf. Ez 32:7

Is 50:3

made eternity seem to be death.

All this was 'the rind of the pomegranate', but beneath these clouds and under this rind, hidden within for you, our Lord and God, lay strength, wisdom, confidence, gladness, contentment and eternity. In your compassion for us, you broke that rind, and now they lie revealed to us as well, but only in part. By your grace, before us lie revealed the seeds of life, to make us live, to calm our passions, to quench our thirst, to heal our griefs, lighten our labors, encourage us to virtue, solace us with its joy. Here on earth, though the face of heaven may still be overcast, those lowering skies are a sign to us of serenity, not of storm. They betoken God's covenant, not his wrath, his grace, not his indignation. O God, we know you are faithful to your debts, true to your undertakings, rich and splendid in making repayment. You have said, you have gone surety, you have sworn, that when you cover the skies with clouds,
Cf. Gen 9:4 you are giving us a sign of your covenant.* Yes, Lord, this is what you have done, and we marvel at it, we rejoice, and give you thanks for it, all of us who fear you and believe in your love for us.

It is clear enough that it is to such people and not to others, there is made this solemn promise and sign of your covenant. For, as the prophet says, 'you have given those who fear you a sign, to flee from the sight of the bow,
Ps 60:4 that your loved ones may be safe.'* In fact, it is when you cover yourself with these heavy storm clouds and conceal from them your majesty and serenity, that you have bent

and prepared your bow.* It is precisely *Cf. Ps 7:13* because on that day you suffered yourself to be judged that from that day on you will have the right to sit in judgement. It is when you humbly took your place in the court of a strange judge, waiting patiently for your sentence and receiving it joyously, that you 'set up your throne in judgement'.* Yes, my *Cf. Ps 9:7* king and my God, it was then that you bent your bow, proclaiming even to your enemies themselves, though in a very hidden way, that one day they would see 'the Son of man coming in the clouds of heaven.'* You were *Mt 26:64* referring, of course, to the last day, the day of your wrath, when you will come with outstretched bow and with your deadly weapons, the arrows you have made into shafts of fire.* *Cf. Ps 7:14*

7. But the dark and burning hues that are the dominant colors in this visible bow, whenever these clouds blot out our heaven, are unmistakable evidence of tears continually flowing, as if of a perpetual flood and an eternal conflagration. But this is only for those to whom it is given to understand, that is, those who are prepared to be afraid. Clearly, when they flee from the sight of the outstretched bow, the sign of God's anger, they make it a sign of covenant, quickening their flight before they experience the death-dealing arrow. Indeed, it will be too late to fly when harsh winter has already begun and the sabbath rest makes it impossible.* *Cf. Mt 24:20*

Indeed excessive pain, like some stormy winter, the prelude to death allows of no other thoughts but of its own unrestrained bitterness. It leaves no room for repentance, for it concentrates all a man's thoughts and feelings on itself. Accordingly, a soul taking its leave of this life, as though on some day of rest, during which it is forbidden to set its hand to any further works of merit, can do nothing now except be at leisure. Yes, but the leisure only holds it back from what would be useful, not from what distresses, disturbs and torments it. O winter, with your storms and lightning, O sabbath of sorrow and distress, O outstretched bow that is never to be bent again, O arrow with your wound that can never be healed!

8. But what has this to do with us? The Lord our God has sworn, and it would be wicked not to believe in him. For the godless, these are signs of death that lead to death, but for us, the bow is bent so that we may flee, and the arrow is got ready to prevent our being killed.* On any day that the bow appears to me in the clouds of heaven, I have the chance to acknowledge, with deep reverence, that Jesus was judged for my sake. That sign gives me new life, and I have no doubt at all that it signifies God's covenant with me. It tells me that when he comes to judge the world with fire, the Lord will remember me* and remember his covenant.†

Cf. Ps 7:14

**Cf. Responsory to lection nine in the Office of the Dead.*

†Cf. Lev 26:42

On that day, too, the heavens will be overcast with clouds, but with clouds of a totally different kind. They will be clouds of wrath and anger, and they will seem to blot out the tranquil majesty of God's countenance. Indeed, on these clouds there will clearly appear a bow, and it will even be one that cannot be bent, a bow of rigid severity. Yet, even when this is how it shows itself, the bow will be a sign of God's covenant for all who love him. Whatever his anger towards his enemies, he will remember his compassion for his friends,* and the day that will be one of extreme sternness for the hostile, will likewise be a day of everlasting covenant for those he loves. *Cf. Hab 3:2*

9. But now, let us come back to 'the bride's cheeks', although what we have said about the spouse is, generally speaking, not unconnected with his praise of his bride. In fact, when he compares her cheeks to the rind of a pomegranate, he is likening them, as we have already pointed out, to his own cheeks, and even the spouse himself could not think of likening them to anything finer or braver or more lovable. By his grace, we have pointed out what is meant by both 'cheeks', by 'pomegranate', by 'rind of pomegranate', and even by 'broken pieces of pomegranate'. What we still have to do is discuss the bride's 'secrets', about which the spouse adds a phrase: 'concealing your secrets.'* *Sg 6:6*

10. Like a practised speaker, with an exceptional skill in eulogizing, he passes over those hidden qualities in his praise, so that by keeping them hidden, he in fact shows them as above such praise. The concealment is the loudest proclamation. And so, by 'the bride's cheeks', admiration is expressed for her reserve and patience. Following the teaching and the example of her beloved, she gives these cheeks to those who pluck them,* she gives them to those who spit upon them,* she gives them to be ill-treated and insulted, as soon as one is

Cf. Is 50:6
Ibid.

Cf. Mt 5:39 struck, offering the other.* In the sight of men, these things are great indeed. But if they were not animated by the Spirit of love in her heart, they would immediately become—I do not say, something little, but—nothing at all! 1 Cor 13:4 For, 'charity is patient.'* Otherwise, without charity, however much suffering there may be, it has no right to be called 'patient'. Rather than resembling this kind of cheek, it will be the cheekbone of an ass, a spiritless bone, a lifeless bone, dry and parched. It has nothing at all in common with these cheeks, that make the bride so worthy of her spouse's love and admiration.

11. Two colors blend within the bride's cheeks to make them beautiful, namely, a radiant white and redness. There is a whiteness, making her aware within herself of her purity and innocence, through which she endures her persecutors and calumniators. There is a redness, and so, despite all her innocence, she blushes as if repentant, and the more freely she endures everything, the more does she have in common with her spouse. In the end, she too can say, 'Now Ps 69:5 I have restored what I never stole.'* These two colors, glowing in the bride's cheeks, endow her face with a wonderful beauty and draw her spouse's heart to love, and the more he sees this love is hidden, the holier he considers it.

However, this innocence will not be truly innocent unless she gives up all desire to harm even those who persecute her, and her modesty will not be pleasing unless she tries her best to feel pleasure also in those who envy her glory. But this is what the bride says: 'When we are cursed, we bless.'* And again, 'Have I ever requited those who did me wrong?'* She says this, too, 'With those who hate peace, I am a peace maker.'* And elsewhere, 'Lord, do not lay this sin to their charge.'* For the spouse declares, 'Bless those who persecute you.'* I put it to you, what virtue can you think of that is more 'secret' than this one, and yet, what could be holier or more wonderful?

1 Cor 4:13

Ps 7:5

Ps 120:6

Acts 7:60

Mt 5:44

12. Your witnesses* are wonderful, Lord Jesus, and so the soul of your bride examines them with great attention. It is because of the witness you have given that she herself becomes wonderful and lovable in your sight. Your witness is the true witness, and without it, all other witnesses are nothing at all, as the apostle tells us.* Without it, there would be nothing precious in the death of your martyrs,* but their witness would be no more than the death of sheep and cattle. But the bone of your secret witness, which you fashioned in secret* for your loved ones who love you in return, you have hidden in secret.* You have given your loved ones the gift of your secret love, so that, amid the fires of persecution, they never cease to burn with this love for their persecutors. In our day, these witnesses are very rare, and yet, by the grace of the only Son of God, our day is not completely without them. The time of the grape harvest, when the winepress of the church overflowed with the precious blood of the grape, that time has gone for good, but still, by God's mercy, it can be seen that a

martyria

Cf. 1 Cor 13:3, Bernard, SC 47.5; SBOp 2:64; CF 31:7.

**Cf. Ps 116:13*

Cf. Ps 139:14

Ibid.

bunch of grapes hangs on the vine. In the turmoil of everyday life, we are continually experiencing new winepresses, and he who treads out the vintage is at hand! The vineyard belongs to the beloved, as Isaiah says, the vineyard was made for the beloved,* and the only wine he expects from it is the wine of love, to be stored in his wine cellar to give drink to himself and his bride.* The blood of this grape is of the purest, and they refuse to drink from the product of any other vine.*

Cf. Is 5:1

Cf. Sg 1:4

Cf. Deut 32:14

May he be close to this vineyard and this wine, for to him belong the plantation and the work. And may we be pleasing to him in them both, through our earnest desire for genuine love of him, who lives and reigns with

God the Father and the Holy Spirit,
one God, for ever and ever.
Amen.

SERMON FIFTY-FOUR

The beginning of the fifty-fourth sermon. Of the three kinds of holy men, namely, prelates, who are called 'queens', and those who, consecrated to God, keep themselves wholly for him, and these are called 'concubines', and others of the faithful who are humble and have the title 'maidens'. Also there is a discussion of the unity of the church, as much with reference to the authority of the holy see as to the humble devotion to it of all the church.

'THERE ARE sixty queens, and eighty concubines, and maidens without number. One is my dove, one is my perfect one, the only one of her mother, the favorite of her who bore her.'* *Sg 6:7,8*

After generously commending his bride, making a careful and orderly study of everything in her that is lovely and deserves praise, the spouse suddenly shifts to a different style. This is, to compare the bride with distinguished women, and by doing this, make it obvious to everybody, what a privileged position is hers, and what unique glory. Therefore, queens, concubines and maidens are brought before us and their dignity and plurality are explicitly mentioned. Then, in contrast to them all, the bride is singled out for a fourfold honor, that of being called 'one', that is, unique, as well as being described as 'dove', 'perfect one', and 'favorite'.

On the surface, the superficial meaning of this verse, its 'skin', is very dry, and anyone childish enough to swallow it down without thinking, disposed to marvel at and hanker after the pleasure which Solomon, who wrote it, must have had in the number of his queens and concubines, has tied himself down to 'the letter that kills'.* But though for Christ's sake all these things are reckoned as refuse, seeing that we are adults, the same table of carnal pleasures is spread first, so that over it may be laid the table of the new Solomon, arrayed with fresh delights. In this way our refreshment may be seen the more wonderful when the two are compared, the former appearing in their true light as refuse, the latter as true and chaste delights.

2 Cor 3:6

So, when we each take our places at this banquet truly great, we must look carefully, as Solomon of old advised, at what is set before us at that feast.* We must pull aside the veil of shameful love, that caused that first Solomon to make peace with those who sought after his soul,* and to tarnish his own reputation, enervated by so many women. Under the guidance of the Holy Spirit, we must set ourselves to draw out the very core of sacred love.

Cf. Pr 23:1

Cf. Ps 120:6

2. So it seems to me that these three types of woman are meant to stand for three types of soul, cleaving to Christ, the true Solomon, by virtue of three types of holiness. First are those who are called to the government of souls, and who carry it out purely and

faithfully. The second type are those who have abandoned the enticements of this world to be attentive to the holy repose of interior peace.* And the third type are those who, humbly submissive to their pastors, walk in the paths of holiness, having learned from the chief shepherd to attend more to what their shepherds say than what they do.*

Cf. Gilbert, SC 1:2; PL 184:13; CF 14:45.

Cf. Mt 23:3

Those who have a pure vocation and have reached the pastoral office, have every right to be called 'queens'. They discharge their office with a pure intention, not seeking in it the things that are their own, not seeking glory, not seeking riches, not seeking pleasure, but seeking the things that are their spouse's.* In other words, they seek the glory of being zealous in God's honor, and the usefulness of bringing forth and rearing spiritual sons. Certainly, men like this deserve also to be called 'kings', because of their fatherly care and selfless vigor in showing regal impartiality. But they are still 'queens', because of their motherly disposition, and the gentleness and tenderness that are characteristic of a mother's dealing with her sons. See whether this is not the famous promise made by God to the church through Isaiah: 'Kings will be your foster fathers, and queens your nursing mothers.'* Notice how expressly and magnificently, as much for the church's glory as for the honor of those who rear her, the church is told, so many years in advance, that those who fulfil the office of rearing her, will share in the glory of her regal dignity.

Cf. 1 Cor 13:5

Is 49:23

3. But oh, how the church suffers in these days from the neglect of her foster

fathers and nursing mothers! How tragic for her babes and sucklings! When sucklings turn to the breasts, they are dry, and when babes ask for bread, there is no one to give it to
Lam 4:4 them.* The office of nursing is held cheap in the church, held cheap indeed by both nurslings and nurses, and oh, cheapest of all by those who know how to bare the breast and pour milk even into the mouths of the children who refuse to make an effort. For the rest, though they think little or not at all of the care or tenderness or love that are natural for a foster parent, when it comes to regal arrogance, to glory and exaltation, they neglect nothing, they leave nothing undone and let nothing pass. No, even more than the great apostles, 'the strong gods of the
Ps 47:9 earth are powerfully raised on high.'*

Although they do not act as foster parents, then, they still reign, but not with the apostles; they reign, but not from God's power or with God's presence. The apostle says, 'You have become kings, but without
1 Cor 4:8 us,'* and the Lord says, 'They have reigned
Hos 8:4 as kings, but not through me.'* Queens like this, therefore, are also concubines. They are queens because of their popular superiority and the severity of their autocratic rule; they are concubines because of the excess of their impudent lack of shame.

4. But let us leave all who are like this, clearly so far away from the bedchamber of our Solomon that the mere hearing of something about him causes them distaste. Let us return to those who receive these names for a happier reason, and are called 'queens' because

they bear and nurse sons for their heavenly spouse. Others are called 'concubines', because they repose solely in his love, quite content simply to enjoy him, without too eager a desire to give birth to children. This is why it is appropriate that the number 'sixty' should be assigned to the first, and 'eighty' to the second, because when a group of ten is multiplied by a group of six, it contains a symbolic guarantee of double perfection. The number 'ten' contains the ten commandments of the law, and by it is signified perfect knowledge of the commandments. But the number 'six' symbolizes the climax of God's creative work and was bestowed by God on the works of man,* and so is a symbol of the perfection of a good day's work. *Cf. Gen 1:32*

And so there are sixty queens who are also nursing mothers, that is, who feed at both their breasts the sons they have borne for Christ, and these breasts are holy words and good work. Because of this they await the reward of a glorious recompense, the placing on their head of the crown of the kingdom,* when they are set over all the possessions of their spouse.* For those who do, and teach men to do the same, will be called great, scripture tells us, in the kingdom of heaven.* What greater invitation or more splendid title could there be, than to be called kings and queens of heaven?

Cf. Est 2:17
Cf. Mt 24:47
Cf. Mt 5:19

The concubines have a glory of a lower order, but it is all they desire. Here on this earth, they have the blessed firstfruits of bliss in their beloved Solomon, and they await the full consummation of this bliss when his glory is revealed. And it is for this reason that they are set down as being eighty in number, precisely because the eighth is the day of resurrection, and it is for that day they strive to make themselves ready, by meditation on God's law.

5. Finally, there are the humble souls who are called 'maidens', those whose value is held in low esteem by those who give an impression of over-elevated 'spirituality'.* Indeed, it is our custom to speak of them as being 'without number', meaning that we usually have little esteem for their ability to achieve anything. Hence, 'The maidens are without number'* either 'in the thoughts of the prosperous,'* or in their own eyes. The result is only to bring them all the more nobly into the reckoning of him 'who numbers the great throng of the stars'* and 'calls into being that which has no being',* the less they are reckoned of any consequence in the sight of men.

Cf. Rom 11:20

Sg 6:7

Job 12:5

Ps 147:4

Rom 4:17

It is one of this number that we hear speaking in the psalm: 'I am young and despised.'* Despised indeed, because of 'the scorn of the prosperous and the contempt of the proud',* who despise my youth. But much more am I despised and despicable in my own opinion, remembering how I once went away from my father into a distant land, taking with me my share of the inheritance.*

Ps 119:141

Ps 123:4

Cf. Lk 15:13

6. Therefore, 'queens', 'concubines' and 'maidens' stand for three types of holy men. The first kind are profitable to others in word and example, the second are already making

very great progress in working out their own salvation, and the third are the humble and contrite, unskilled in holy warfare, and as yet unworthy to experience anything at all of the sweetness of spiritual consolation. To all of these the spouse makes it quite clear, singling her out for special commendation, that he prefers his beloved. Yet he does not name her, so as to make it possible for us too, to wonder at her, to praise and imitate her. O Lord, my God, who is she, and we shall praise her?* For you esteem her as beyond the limitations of human virtue, since you have lifted her to a height beyond that of 'queens'. *Cf. Sir 31:9*

7. Why do you want to make her greater than a queen? But I seem to hear you answering me, that queen differs from queen in charity. And with respect to the church, who is the great and special bride of Christ, an easy explanation presents itself, that it is she who hears her spouse say, in the truest and most special sense, 'One is my dove, one is my perfect one.'* Certainly, one dove, because of the complete simplicity of faith, one perfect one, because her love alone is perfect. Strong and unshaken the church stands, and will stand from age to age, resting secure on two foundations, namely, universal truth and unshakeable love for God and her sons. *Sg 6:8*

Yes, the 'pegs of this tabernacle'* have been well soldered together, though the wickedness of so many different heretics has tried to shatter them to pieces. They have been fixed so firmly by the mighty hand of the omnipotent God, that the hand of man is *Cf. Ex 38:31* utterly unable to wrench them free, but only destroys itself in its passionate attempts. But as well as this, the church is surrounded on all sides by cords of mutual love, and in her various needs, she has various helps to offer herself. Within the limits of the different gifts that result from the variety of graces, she is never slow in turning to herself with a view to mutual services.*

Cf. 1 Cor 12:5

Therefore, the word of truth, which the Father of our Lord Jesus placed on Peter's lips, will never be taken away from Peter's lips.* And likewise, for all eternity it will never cease to be on the lips of Peter's descendants. So if any one has a doubt about any part of his faith, he has a ready means of putting his question to the Lord, in the successors of Peter, and he will receive his answer from the mercy-seat, from between the wings of the cherubim.* For we are not demanding proof that it is Christ who is speaking* to us from 'his holy place'.† If we are truly sons of God,* then we are not reluctant to admit that we are also sons of his beloved bride. On the contrary, just as we are determined to honor our Father, so are we equally determined to honor our mother, lovingly and humbly, so that 'it may be well with us'* and we may 'possess a blessing with our inheritance'.*

Cf. Mt 16:18
Cf. Ex 25:20
**Cf. Lk 10:16*
†Cf. Ps 108:7
**Cf. 1 Jn 3:2*
Cf. Deut 5:16
Cf. 1 Pet 3:9

8. We admit, then, we make no secret of it, that 'truly the Lord is in this place'.* This earth is truly 'his footstool',* and however much a man yearns for the things of heaven, there is no other way to get there except from this earth of ours. It is to this earth that, every

Gen 28:16
Cf. Is 66:1

hour, there is an untiring coming and going of angels. They rise and descend, presenting the church's prayers to the ears of her spouse, as well as speeding to declare the spouse's secrets to his bride. Just as long ago in the past, the place the Lord chose for himself was in Jerusalem, and he would accept no sacrificial gift or prayer at all, from anywhere other than from 'his temple in Jerusalem',* so it is in these last days, too. Now that the light of utter Truth has shone forth from the midst of the darkness made by shadows,* the Wisdom of God has appointed one place in this world for his church, as if as the capital city of his entire kingdom. Courageously and wisely, he has entered the strong man's house and the very home of wickedness has had its head cut off.* In the place characterized by total untruth and complete pride and emptiness and universal lack of trust, he laid down the claims of his own sovereignty and he made it the capital city of his pride, who is all purity. He changed the bit of error, which was in the people's jaw, for the bit of government, holy and prudent, so that they could guide all peoples.

Cf. Ps 68:29

Cf. Jn 1:5

Cf. Jdth 13:10

So, just as there is one Lord and one faith,* so from and under the one Lord of all, there is one head for the one church. Under this one head, then the church herself is one, uniting herself and humbly cleaving to her head. Henceforth she strives with all her strength to conform herself to him, above and below, on the right hand and on the left, on every side and in every place, so as to complete and maintain, in every single one of her members,

Cf. Eph 4:5

the oneness of her sacred body.

In the church, therefore, the church of Rome, is the Lord's chief altar, in the defense of the practice of the faith. In the church are the tables of the covenant, they are ready for her to spread abroad. In the church is the manna of heaven, in the oblation of her Lord's body, so that the ceremony of this one, same sacrament can never be impaired by age or neglect. In the church is the rod of Aaron, held in readiness to avenge all disobedience. (Among so many rods, it is chosen to be the only one that has flowered
Cf. Num 17:8 and brought forth fruit,* so that everyone is in authority, and most of all he who holds Aaron's place and executes the duty of high priesthood, when he has of necessity to strike with the rod, may in the first place, hold this wonder up for view: the wonder of his rigor that flowers into mercy, and from that flower breaks into the fruit of salvation.) Furthermore, in that church is the ark of the covenant, that is, the faithful receptacle of God's wisdom and knowledge. There, too, is the mercy-seat, namely, the supreme power of showing mercy to the sins and transgressions of the penitent. There are the cherubim of
Cf. Ex 37:9 glory, namely, the power of the angels,* which, after the pattern of the church that
Cf. Eph 2:6 is 'in the heavenly places',* hand over to the universal church, by God's will, all these things, sending them by the hand of Peter, as
Cf. Lev 8:36 if it were the hand of Moses.*

But what is the purpose of all we have spoken of? Surely to demonstrate the wisdom of the Word, and to give us a fuller understanding of why he praises his bride in these terms: 'The only one of her mother, the favorite of her who bore her.'* *Sg 6:8*

9. 'The only one', he says, 'of her mother.' But, we may ask, why is she this to her mother? She is this simply because she is, being completely devoted to her mother, owing her, after God, everything that is according to God's will. She acknowledges that she draws vigor from her spirit, that she lives by her faith, is enlightened by her knowledge, sanctified by her merits, purified by her godliness, and she hopes to enter heaven's bliss through her charity. This is certainly why he also says, 'the favorite of her who bore her.'* Ibid. Whatever grace and favor she possesses, or even whatever bliss and glory she thinks she will one day possess, she attributes it all to the great loving kindness of 'her who bore her'. This is why the great princes of the church utter that glorious cry: 'He chose for us his heritage, the pride of Jacob whom he loved.'* *Ps 47:4* Clearly, for these first fathers of ours and for their sons, those who were born in place of these fathers and were made princes,* *Cf. Ps 45:17* the 'favorite chosen one' is she of whom it is said, 'The favorite of her who bore her',* *Sg 6:8* the 'heritage of God', the 'pride of Jacob', the beautiful bride of the Lord Jesus. Yes, she is the favorite chosen for them, but not chosen by them, for both she and they have One who does the choosing, and also the loving, One who, before time began, chose them as well as loved them.

Yet, when the spouse says that the whole church is 'the favorite of her who bore her',

it comes ringing from his lips in great praise of the principal church, the church of Rome, the mother who bears us all. This is obviously what we read the spouse promising her in another place: 'As I live, says the Lord, you shall put them all on as an ornament, you shall
Is 49:18 bind them on as does a bride.'* Or rather, these words redound, all the same, to the praise of the humility and devotion of the whole church, which attributes the grace of its election, first to its source and Lord, and then to its mother. Although not chosen favorite by her, it is chosen for her, and she is the reason for its being chosen, by the grace and generosity of her spouse, who with

God the Father and the Holy Spirit,
lives and reigns God,
for ever and ever.
Amen.

SERMON FIFTY-FIVE

The beginning of the fifty-fifth sermon. That the lovers of Jesus are of two types, here called 'queens and concubines', and there is a third type, not yet proficient in love, but nevertheless on fire to practise this holy warfare. After this comes a discussion of the soul that loves God perfectly, and longs with entire devotion for the things of heaven.

'THERE ARE SIXTY QUEENS, and eighty concubines, and maidens without number. One is my dove, one is my perfect one, the only one of her mother, the favorite of her who bore her.'* *Sg 6:7,8*

I am well aware that you are waiting for a second serving of this verse, and that you hope for a meal for our own community, since what was said yesterday had the praise of the church as its main object. For my part, I am glad to meet your expectations, but you, on your part, must pray that what I produce is not unworthy of so great a theme and that you will profit from it.

In my opinion, then, 'queens', 'concubines' and 'maidens' are meant to signify three kinds of lovers. The first kind, eager for perfection, strive to hasten to perfection by the straight and narrow way.* The second kind, who have experience of Christ's love,* follow him in *Cf. Mt 7:14* *Cf. RB 58:8* sweet and gentle ways. But the third kind, who have as yet no interior knowledge of the sweetness of Christ, have all the same an ardent longing to obey and to practise this holy warfare. So they run swiftly with the others, and come at last to possess the same reward.

2. Obviously, the first kind are thought worthy to be called 'queens', because, having entered on the royal road, they think it intolerable to have to wait upon the future: they have the joy of understanding something of what the kingdom of Christ means and they hasten, even here below, to reign with
Cf. 2 Tim 2:12 him.* They say: His kingdom is certainly
Jn 18:37 not 'of this world',* yet, all the same, it is 'in this world'. For the kingdom of God and his Christ is 'righteousness and peace and joy in
Rom 14:17 the Holy Spirit'*, and anyone who is privileged to share in these things, already 'reigns
Cf. Rev 20:4 with God'.*

For the time being, I can think of those kinds of perfection (perhaps there are more than three, but I am anxious to share with you things as they appear to me at present). I hear, I read it in the gospels, that when the Lord Jesus preached the good news of the kingdom of God, he said that the blessed
Cf. Mt 5:3 ones were the poor,* and those who suf-
Cf. Mt 5:10 fered persecution for justice' sake,* and to both of these, he did not 'promise' the kingdom of heaven, but he placed it right in their lap. If what we hear is true, or rather, since it must be true, being the words of Truth Himself, then these two classes of men are here and now in possession of the kingdom. They are kings, and not of some trifling princi-

pality, but of the kingdom of which the Lord our God is also king.

3. But a poverty so glorious: what do you think can be its nature? Surely it is one that seeks to possess nothing as its own, has no ambition for worldly success, does not strive after the seats of honor,* does not hunt for applause from its admirers,* has no inflated esteem for the resounding titles of this world's great ones. No, for the love of the glory of heaven, it holds in disdain everything which savors of vanity. When these works of the gospel ring in your ears, brothers, surely such a joyous message should make you lift up your heads? All that could prevent you—which God forbid!—would be the possibility of your not having received, up to now, 'the Spirit which is from God' so as to know, as the apostle puts it, 'the gifts that have come to us from God'.*

Cf. Mt 23:6
Cf. Mt 6:2
Cf. 1 Cor 2:12

Rejoice greatly, exult and sing for joy!* 'Do not fear, little flock, because your Father has been pleased to give you a kingdom.'* I tell you that the Lord has done great things for you.* It would be wrong to be ungrateful, for a single moment, for such a great grace, for 'he has not done so to every nation',* choosing you out so graciously to be his own favored possession. Sing praise to God, then, for what he has done for you, sing praise to him with great happiness!* 'All earth's kings shall praise you, Lord, for they have heard every word from your mouth.'* To what other kings than to you and kings like you, can it be said: 'for they have heard every word from your mouth'? And it is in

Cf. Ps 32:11
Lk 12:32
Cf. Ps 126:2
Ps 147:20
Cf. Ps 47:6
Ps 138:4

order that they may 'praise' that they are
expressly told, 'and they shall sing of the
Lord's ways, for great is the glory of the
Ps 138:5 Lord.'*

Blessed be God! Over the whole world we
see many nations are this kind of kingdom.
We see it, we hear it, we read it in scripture,
just as it was prophesied so long ago: 'For
see, the kings of the earth assembled, they
Ps 48:4 assembled all together.'* And again: 'When
the people come together, and the kings to
Ps 102:22 serve the Lord.'*

4. Again, when they likewise 'suffer perse-
Mt 5:10 cution for justice' sake',* they look for the
crown of the same kingdom, but now repro-
duced with twofold merit, though they do not
so much look for this crown as receive it. Why
should they not have crowns upon their
Cf. Est 2:17 heads?* Not only do they glory in the confi-
dence of God's sons, but they have also
learned from Christ how to rejoice in afflic-
Cf. Rom 5:3 tions.* Paul thought this was so precious a
crown that he says, 'Far be it from me to
glory in anything except the cross of our
Gal 6:14 Lord Jesus Christ.'* Paul rejoiced, then, not
so much in having laid up for him a crown of
Cf. 2 Tim 4:8 justice,* but because that crown was laid upon
him. It has in it many precious stones, just
precisely as many as the stones he received on
earth from the stone-throwers, just precisely
as many as his tortures, his shipwrecks, his
Cf. 2 Cor 11:23-27 imprisonments, chains, perils and labors.*

And we too, dearest brothers, we too have
not been defrauded by God of a share in this
glory. As the same apostle says, 'All who wish
to live godly lives in Christ Jesus, will suffer

persecution.'* I pray that when persecution does threaten, we may not weary of remembering our crown, and that we may be ready to defend bravely the honor of our kingdom, lest any unwillingness to suffer should render us feeble-hearted. My hope is that, under threat of persecution, we should rather rejoice and exult* as befits kings, seeing that we can be certain of reigning, only when we realize that our heart is in the right hand of God, where the heart of kings is.*

2 Tim 3:12

Cf. Rev 19:7

Cf. Sir 10:2

5. But there is also the third kind of perfection, having no less than either of the other kinds, and which the Lord referred to when he said, 'Love your enemies, do good to those who hate you, so that you may be the sons of your Father who is in heaven.'* And a little later: 'You are to be perfect, just as your heavenly Father is perfect.'* This is, of course, a high and arduous path, but it leads to the heights. This is the 'more excellent path of charity', one that is not only long-suffering, but also warm and generous.*

Mt 5:44

Mt 5:48

Cf. 1 Cor 12:32

So then, brothers, as well as the gifts of grace already mentioned, we must be zealous for this most precious of all the gifts,* so as to make 'our sun rise upon those who hate us.'* Our 'sun' is our charity, warm with benevolence and radiant with practical kindness. We shall indeed prove ourselves truly 'sons of our Father who is in heaven',* if so great a light glows within us that we are eager to show ourselves heirs of our Father's charity. What is your opinion? Would you not agree that in this way, too, we are kings, because we are sons of the Most High?* Are

Cf. 1 Cor 13:13

Cf. Mt 5:45

Cf. Mt 4:8

Cf. Ps 82:6

we not kings if we imitate our Father's perfection and on this earth set up the kingdom of charity?

6. But how tragic it is! All too often, cowardice crushes our ignoble spirits, and our kingdom is hardly ever free from strife and civil discord. It is heartrending that so constantly clouds blot out our sun, so that usually the light of our face does not fall on those who have done us some little injury. Nearly every hour, even in the easiest instances, we run the risk of having the sun 'go
Cf. Eph 4:26 down upon our anger'.* But in us it is evident how far we are from the glory of those 'queens' who were bound to Solomon by holy wedlock, because they learned from
Cf. Mt 5:25 Solomon,* that with those who hate peace,
Cf. Ps 120:7 they must make peace.*

7. Finally, it is of these that scripture speaks earlier as 'encompassing the couch of
Sg 3:7 Solomon, holding swords and expert on war.'* Obviously the number sixty, which is found in both places, makes it unmistakably clear that in both places the same people are being referred to. But there are described as encompassing the couch of Solomon with swords, and here they are represented as entering that couch, since they are queens. The intention is to make it plain to every soul that longs for interior peace, the very great eagerness, the courageous and tireless warfare that is needed to 'encompass' that couch. From their Solomon, therefore, these queens bear noble sons, destined very soon to be a mighty nation, the inheritors of a renowned inheritance. They
Cf. Lk 6:20 proceed from poverty into a deeper poverty,*

from endurance to a deeper endurance,* from charity to a deeper charity,* but never do they approach the couch of their Solomon without bearing away from it some fruitful blessing.

Cf. Rom 5:4
Cf. 1 Jn 3:16

8. Likewise, the concubines, though not aware of so great a glory, do nevertheless themselves share in this same happiness, though less frequently and in a less sublime way. Certainly, they are distinguished from the queens by their charity, but all the same, they are made one through their charity. By virtue of their greater zeal, the queens enjoy their spouse more frequently and delightfully, as their own legal husband, and there are what one might call spiritual perceptions which, like sons, they are privileged to bear and bring up for him. But in whatever way the care for their brother's souls is entrusted to them, they feel for them a mother's love. They labor lovingly to bring them to birth, so that Christ may be more fully formed in them.*

Cf. Gal 4:19

But the concubines have less of this Spirit of understanding, which would enable them to bring forth sons of such noble birth. They know Christ 'according to the flesh',* and they are still inclined to be very tenderly attached, with what is really a fleshly attachment, to whatever he did while in the flesh, and it is things of this nature that they are anxious to read and hear.* It is in virtue of these things that they exercise their spirit in meditating about Jesus, that they lift up clean hands to implore the sight of Jesus, that they season and soothe their dispositions, as if with an ingenious salve, when pain or

1 Cor 10:18

**Cf. Bernard,* SC *20:8; SBOp 1:120; CF 4:154.*

bitterness assails them, that, rather as though with a war-horn and battle trumpet, they winnow their enemies, and blow them all away.* [*Cf. Ps 44:3*]

The number eighty is very apt for them, for this is the number of Abraham's years when, at God's call, he went out from Haran to enter upon the ways of perfection.* [*Cf. Gen 12:4*] For them, too, the favor of this call from God is the prologue to great perfection, and provided that no difficulties exhaust them and call them back, they are close to sharing with Abraham in the promised land and being fed with the inheritance of Jacob.* [*Deut 32:9*]

9. And then, we have the 'maidens', who, as we said above, have as yet tasted nothing of the savor of interior love. It is of one of this number that it is said, later on, 'We have a little sister, and she has no breasts.'* [*Sg 8:8*] This is also why it is said that they are 'without number',* [*Sg 6:8*] because up to now, the solitariness of their single state confines them, and they have not come to the state of holy matrimony, in which there are two. For scripture says of the married, 'They shall be two in one flesh.'* [*Gen 2:24*] And again, 'If two lie together, they are warm',* [*Sir 4:11*] to which it adds, 'How can one who is alone, be warm?'* [Ibid.] 'It is better, therefore,' as it says in the same place, 'to be two than one.'* [*Sir 4:9*] For, 'Woe to the one who is alone!'* [*Sir 4:10*]

The single state of the maidens, then, is lonely, because it has no right to enter, with the queens and concubines, into the secrets of the royal marriage chamber and obtain the embrace and the kiss of Solomon. But they bear the banners of high hope, and during the period when they are growing up to a marriageable age, they begin to adapt and adjust themselves to their future spouse. Already, too, they draw an occasional sigh of love, and although they still make their beds far from the threshold of the marriage chamber, they secretly turn over in their hearts the first stirrings of charity. 'Let him kiss me with the kiss of his mouth.'* And again: 'At all times, my soul is consumed with longing for your decrees.'*

Sg 1:1

Ps 119:20

But if, in all seriousness, the desire for this holy kiss allures the maidens, and they long to taste for themselves its sweetness, then they must gird their loins with courage* and leave behind the dangerous and wanton ways of youth. It is characteristic of youth to scrutinize all that can be seen, as well as marveling over all they have seen. At the time of youth, when the character is still being formed, it is natural to be over-eager about outings, to be curious about finding out what is happening, to be restless to roam around, Youth is avid for jesting, intolerant of silence. impatient for peace. It runs away from discipline, eager to be led astray and ready to do the leading! This is why Solomon said: 'Youth and pleasure are vanity.'*

Cf. Pr 31:17

Sir 11:10

Moreover, when youth is converted to more purposeful pursuits, there, too, a very great danger lies in wait, for it cannot distinguish when fervor is too extreme. In fact, since it cannot brook the guiding-rein of greater maturity, it dialogues solely with its own fervor. As Solomon points out, it will

Cf. Pr 15:12 not go to 'the wise',* and it scorns to listen
Cf. Pr 1:8 to standards of its mother,* and so, perhaps, it is for this reason that it is said, 'maidens
Sg 6:7 without number.'* The maidens have no considered plan for what must be done, they have no well-founded measure of judgement. They are moved, not by judgement at all, but only by impulse. Now, in the scriptures, we not infrequently find 'numbers' spoken
Cf. Jer 11:13 of as plans and measures and proportions.* It follows, that, if the maidens are to become ready for love, they must gird up both their loins, strip off all the attitudes of indiscretion, and take on the whiteness proper to the reverend hairs of a riper age. In the same way, to prevent themselves from being carried away by over-eagerness, they must set themselves to do everything with 'number and weight and
Cf. Wis 11:21 measure'.*

But I have said enough about 'queens, concubines and maidens'.

10. But who is it who ranks before all of them? Where in fact, is she, my brothers, and who in fact is she? Surely we do not have to say of her what we read in scripture about wisdom, that 'she is hidden from the eyes of
Job 28:21 all that live',* and we have only heard tell of
Cf. Job 28:22 her?* Equally, surely the spouse does not 'run aimlessly or box like a man beating the
1 Cor 9:26 air',* so as to praise and extol so emphatically somebody who is nowhere to be found? No, no, unthinkable! She is there right enough, though hidden from us; she is there for the holy angels, she is there for her beloved! Although there are few of her, compared to the number of queens and

concubines and 'maidens without number', there is nevertheless not just one of her, but several, and this we tenderly believe and hope with all our heart. Why should we, from our nothingness, limit the hand of the Most High? Why should we dare, from our spiritual tepidity, to hold back, measure out and sit in judgement on the glory of the saints? The spouse asserts, in short, that she is 'one',* but not that she is alone. *Sg 6:8*

11. 'One is my dove,' he says, 'one is my perfect one.'* In other words, she is 'one', *Sg 6:8* because she can concentrate her whole occupation, her whole thought, her whole concern, uniquely on her beloved. This is not for her something optional, it is 'the one thing necessary'.* At the very beginning, when love *Lk 10:42* was just taking root, it was to some extent no more than an option, but persistent desire and repeated experimental knowledge has made it a necessity. For this reason Jesus absolved Mary from her sister's complaint, on the grounds of 'necessity', so that Martha might submit patiently to what had become necessary for Mary.* *Cf. Lk 10:41*

Yes, blessed above all women is she* (and *Cf. Lk 1:42* it can be anyone), who considers that she knows nothing except Christ Jesus,* and *Cf. 1 Cor 2:2* does one thing only: forgets what is behind and stretched herself always to what lies ahead.* For, whatever is behind, however little *Cf. Phil 3:13* it was, she recalls having sensed about Jesus, and so she pours out to him, from the depths of her heart, sighs like those of a dove, because of her imperfect love.

12. She sighs, because she has not yet

come to a pure love for her spouse, so uniquely lovable, so completely desirable. She sighs over his absence, sighs, too, over his presence. But when he is absent, her sigh-
Cf. Ps 38:9 ing is not hidden from him.* Indeed, so little is it hidden, that from the depths of his sanctuary, from his resting place in the Father's bosom, she impetuously draws him down to her. All the same, in this matter it is not importunity that wins the victory, it is charity. Charity is not importunate, though it is impetuous, and in fact, it exerts a stronger pressure than importunity does, though more gently. It uses a gentle force, it draws sweetly, it exerts a pleasant pressure.

On the other hand, when her spouse is present, she sighs no less, but sighs more sweetly. Obviously, she earnestly begs him to stay with her. She urges him to reveal to her
Cf. Ps 119:18 the 'marvels of his law',* she questions him about the glory of his kingdom, she entreats him to let his face shine more brightly. She beseeches him with all the urgency at her command to preserve and perfect what he has begun in her. While he is still with her, she anticipates his departure by asking him to visit her again without delay, after he has gone.

But the dove does not usually breathe these sighs only to herself. She shares her sighing with those who have not yet learned how to sigh like this. She bestows her sighs, too, on those who should be totally given up to sighing and weeping, but instead, sad to say, can only laugh, and so prepare for themselves inconsolable grief. O the bride's charity! It overflows with sighs and tears, it takes into its own home the needy and the homeless,* and washes their feet with her tears.* The bride sees how sadly the city of Jerusalem rejoices in the present day, and how great the sighing that will come down upon it in the day that is coming. 'On that day, its enemies will surround it and straighten it on every side',* and the sight produces a most tender flood of tears from the fountain of tenderness within her. She says, with Jesus, 'If you had but known!'*

Cf. Is 58:7
Cf. Lk 7:44
Lk 19:43
Lk 19:42

So from every side and wherever she looks, she has reason for sighing. She mourns with the weak, she is on fire with those who are made to fall,* she clothes herself in the feelings common to all mankind and enters into their experience, not considering what is her own but what is theirs.* It is aptly said of her, then, 'One is my dove, one is my perfect one,'* because she is wonderfully brought to perfection by this sighing over her own and other men's imperfections. In fact, this is her true perfection: to know and sigh over her own imperfection, to sigh with those who sigh and, as said above, to feel grief on behalf of those who do not sigh.*

Cf. 2 Cor 11:29
Cf. Phil 2:4
Sg 6:8
Cf. Rom 12:15

13. The spouse continues: 'The only one of her mother, the favorite of her who bore her.'* I think that in these words the spouse is specially indicating the charity with which the bride is on fire for the heavenly Jerusalem which is her mother and, indeed, the mother of us all.* This is therefore the mother for whom she is 'the only one', meaning 'the unique one': yearning for her with unique

Sg 6:8
Cf. Gal 4:26

devotion, surrounding her with unique affection. 'Walk all round Jerusalem', she says, 'and surround her.'* Yes, she loves her as a daughter loves her mother, as a nursling loves her nurse. She never forgets that she was formed in her womb and suckled on her milk. She feels grateful to her, because through her instruction she was taught the duties of the faith, through her saving teaching she came to understand the right way to live, and finally, through the example of her charity she learned to love her beloved and through her merits and prayers expects one day to see him fully.

Ps 48:12

14. 'The only one', he says, 'of her mother.'* What is she to her mother except wholly what she is in Christ Jesus? She regards herself as unmistakably depending solely upon what she is in him. This is why one who judged things for what they truly are, said of the wicked man who was lifted up above the cedars of Lebanon: 'I passed by again, and he was gone.'* And another, no less of a contemplative, who also passed by, indeed, who passed into a state above himself, had this to say: 'All the nations are as nothing before him.'* For he alone exists who is eternally and changelessly existant, and every rational soul only truly begins to exist when it starts to cleave, through charity, to him who truly is of himself. So 'to be' really means 'to love', and that is why, as the apostle Jesus loved tells us, 'He who does not love, abides in death.'* Consequently, the bride is to Jesus whatever she is to the mother she reveres, she is certainly no less to her spouse than to her

Sg 6:8

Ps 37:36

Is 40:17

**1 Jn 3:14, Cf. Richard of St Victor,* De Trinitate *5.20; PL 196: 963C.*

mother, or rather, she belongs more completely to them both as she is shared by them both.

Who can unfold the groans, sighs and tears of this daughter to this mother, when she begs her not to turn her face away from her and not to think her unworthy, especially at the very last day when she is summoned? Who can describe the maternal love of this mother for this daughter? Who can speak of the tenderness and charity in her maternal breast, the love with which she yearns towards her daughter, the gentleness with which she opens her bosom to her, inclines her ear, spreads her arms wide? Whose capacity is great enough to ponder over the eager love that keeps her active in her daughter's interests, running with solicitations, now to the Father of the Word, now to the Word of the Father, now to the loving Spirit of them both? For her daughter's sake, her hands are ever extended, stretched out on high to the holy and undivided Trinity. Her hands are not in the least heavy, so that she must sometimes, even for a moment, let them fall before the mother's prayer for her child is heard, or before it is said to this mother, as once to the Canaanite woman: 'Be it done to you as you desire.'* *Mt 15:28*

In consequence, the daughter has, in the affections of 'the one who bore her', the same special place she has in the affections of her spouse. And just as, in his opinion, she is to be ranked before queens, and everyone else who loves him or desires to love him, so too, is she 'the favorite of her who bore her',* *Sg 6:8*

more than all her sisters. Of course, that mother takes her opinion from what she hears, forming it from the expression of her heavenly spouse and taking the rule and measure of her charity from his eternal decrees. May her loving prayers gain for us, also, the compassion of the spouse, the Father's only Son, who
with the Father and the Holy Spirit,
lives and reigns, God,
for ever and ever.
Amen.

SERMON FIFTY-SIX

The beginning of the fifty-sixth sermon. How the church is judged differently by the good and the bad, and which judgement is to receive our fuller assent. Next, what were the beginnings of the church, in what way she shines like the moon or like the sun, and how she will one day be terrible, when she sits in judgement.

'THE DAUGHTERS OF ZION saw her and proclaimed her blessed; the queens and the concubines praised her. Who is this who comes forth, rising like the dawn, fair as the moon, bright as the sun, terrible as an army set in battle array?'* *Sg 6:8.9*

Here, just as in his last words, the spouse enters upon a new day of praising his bride. Almost as if dissatisfied with his own praise, he sets before us the praises of others. When they wonder at his bride and applaud her, he joins his applause to theirs in perfect harmony. He takes the words from their admiring lips, and consecrates them to himself. So we find him seizing upon the expressions of the daughters of Zion, the queens and concubines and including them among his own, since the mantle of praise he is making ready for his bride will be all the more lovely for being woven with the beauty of diversity.* *Cf. Ps 45:9*

He tells us, then, 'The daughters of Zion

Sg 6:8 saw her and proclaimed her blessed.'* Graciously, before embarking on the celebration of another's praise, the spouse first speaks highly of those whose praise he is repeating, especially because it matters a great deal who it is who awards the praise or the blame. It was *Cf. Mt 21:16* from the mouth of babes and sucklings,* where no lie has yet been found, that there came tenderly and sweetly to the ear of *Mt 21:9* Truth: 'Hosanna to the Son of David!'* And when the envious asked him whether he heard *Mt 21:16* what these were saying, he answered, 'Yes!'* Of course, to have 'heard' means to have 'assented to'. But Jesus was assenting to what he himself had inspired in their hearts, and from the pure mouths of the innocent, clearly an apt instrument for the Holy Spirit, he himself drew out the praise of God and the ill-will of his enemies.

Here too, then, there is explicit emphasis on the holiness of those who utter the praises. They are expressly 'daughters of Zion', and not 'daughters of Babylon'! Equally, they are 'queens and concubines', souls who themselves deserve praise, who have the Spirit of God in generous measure. But how each of them differs, and the particular virtues of each in its own class, was discussed in the preceding sermon and need not be repeated.

2. The fact that some arouse the suspicion of being called concubines, who preach *Cf. Phil 1:18* Christ not with pure motives,* but with a view to their own advantage, and cleave to the spouse without sincerity, for example, for the sake of position or means, is wholly out of accord with this canticle. It is wholly

inappropriate both for the praiser and the one who is praised, that the spouse should fashion his praise from the mouths of such as those. Scripture actually tells us: 'A hymn of praise is not fitting on the lips of a sinner.'* We must remember then, that the concubines share in the royal bedchamber, just as the queens do. Granted, they are undoubtedly inferior to them, having not yet advanced to the same degree of charity. But the spouse wisely remarks that those who call the bride blessed, have first seen her.* Otherwise, without this careful viewing of the bride coming first, their enthusiasm would be over-hasty and unreliable. It would be the height of rashness to proclaim what you have not previously investigated, an act of childish folly and careless speech to want to reveal to others something you yourself do not know.

Sir 15:9

Cf. Sg 6:8

3. Those who are used in this affair, therefore, are 'daughters of Zion', not, of course, any of the foolish virgins, but those who attend upon their pure mother with hearts as pure as their bodies, coming to her blessed marriage feast with oil as well as lamps.* Then there are the 'queens and concubines', dignified married women, distinguished by a charity so great that they feel no jealousy about the preference the spouse shows for the bride. Far from being jealous, they are not at all ashamed of marveling at her and extolling her superiority. Very different is the charity of these women from the inveterate envy of Rachel* or the complaint, nonetheless envious, of Martha.* Here, all takes place

Cf. Mt 25:4

Cf. Gen 30:1

Cf. Lk 10:41

in the school of charity* where at once, among the first rudiments, is found the principle of throwing into the heart of the sea all envy and gnashing of teeth,* of burning it with everlasting fire and returning it to its author.* But there is peace and fellowship in the Holy Spirit* for all who love Jesus and her whom he has chosen to be his holy church. However, it is first in praise of her that I must speak to you, since it is she who is the first and special bride of Jesus.

Cf. William, Nat am 9.26; PL 184: 396D; CF 30:86.
**Cf. Ps 46:2*
Cf. Gal 5:21
Cf. 2 Cor 13:13

4. So, 'the daughters of Zion saw her,'* but they do not see in the same way as those who see her with ill-will in their hearts. In fact, these last do not see at all, for their malice blinds them. This is surely what happened to the pharisee who thought he 'saw' Mary, but for two reasons, did not see her.* One was that, before his eyes, she had suddenly changed completely from what he had seen a short time previously, and the other reason was that he had within him 'the leaven of the pharisees'*: he could not see because he was malicious. Jesus said to him, 'Do you see this woman?'* It was as if he said: Yes, you did see a woman, and you think you see her now, but that woman is not this one! Before your eyes she was turned into a new creature, but in your eyes, this has not yet happened.* But it will happen, if the cataract of pride is taken away from your eyes, if the beam of malice is removed,* and if, to cure that cataract, your very great impiety is set beside her very great piety. It will happen on condition that you grow less in your own eyes, and she grows greater.*

Sg 6:8
Cf. Lk 7:39
Cf. Mt 16:6
Lk 7:44
Cf. 2 Cor 5:17
Cf. Mt 7:3
Cf. Jn 3:30

You must ponder devoutly over both love, and the strength of the love, for by it she put off all her old self, and changed from a handmaid of sin to a lover of God, an intimate friend of holiness and a bride of Truth. In this way, with a sort of wonderful liquid eye salve,* Jesus touched the eyes of his host, setting Mary there before his face, all changed in a moment as she was, and setting himself over against his own face, to show how far beneath her he was at present. *Cf. Rev 3:18*

It is on account of men like this, who see so badly, and in fact cannot really see at all, that the church sighs aloud to the Lord her God: 'Those who saw me at a distance, fled from me.'* She says, too, 'They saw me, and they tossed their heads in scorn.'* They tossed their heads to mock me, spurring one another's hearts to malice and contempt. It is with an eye of this kind, which the book of Wisdom tells us is more wicked than anything else in existence, that to this very day they 'see' the church.* They deride her keeping of the sabbath* and say mockingly to one another, 'Is this the city which was called the perfection of beauty, the joy of all the earth?'* But it was the man who looked at her with a more kindly eye who said, 'City of God, glorious things are said of you!'* This is also true of the man who exclaimed, 'The Lord bless you, you pasture of righteousness, you holy hill!'* Moreover, though his eyes were not pure, even Balaam who from far away, gazed at the church under the image of the synagogue, has this to say: 'There is no falsehood in Jacob, no pretence to be

Ps 31:11
Ps 109:25
Cf. Sir 31:15
Cf. Lam 1:7
Lam 2:15
Ps 87:3
Jer 31:23

Num 23:21 seen in Israel.'*

5. Then there was the queen of Sheba. It was not only the appearance of Solomon that so overcame her, that 'there was no more spirit left in her',* but also what she saw. *Cf. 1 Kgs 10:5* Scripture speaks of 'the house that he had built, the food of his table, the seating of his officials and the attendance of his servants, their clothing and their cupbearers, and the burnt offerings he offered in the house of the Lord.'* *1 Kgs 10:4,5* We are told that it was the contemplation of all of these that overwhelmed her, even to the point of ecstasy and it is quite clear that they are meant to symbolize, one by one, the complete beauty of the church, and the different forms of this beauty.

Obviously, the 'house', which is an indivisible and closely linked gathering together of many bricks and beams, stands for the church's unity, of her meeting the one abode of God, in 'the unity of the faith and the knowledge of the Son of God.'* *Eph 4:13* Then the sign and the bond of this unity is the continual sacrifice of the most holy body and blood of the Lord and the feast of catholic teaching, which are symbolized by the 'food of the king's table'. The 'seating of the officials' are the different degrees of religious self-control which each has raised for himself, but at the king's expense and according to Solomon's arrangement. The 'attendance in order of his servants' is what the apostle describes when he speaks of 'some . . . apostles, some evangelists, some prophets, some pastors and teachers, for the work of the ministry, for the building up of the body of

Christ.'* And if they are to be worthy servants of so great a king, it is clear enough that it would not be right to come on duty in workaday clothes. No, they must put on the garments of holiness, as their service requires.* Then there are the 'cupbearers', who go often to the wine cellar and are accustomed to giving joy to king Solomon and the guests at his table by the wine of their charity. Last of all are the 'whole burnt offerings' which are 'offered in the house of the Lord', and these are the fervent prayers of faithful souls. Christ himself told us that the house of God was to be called a house of prayer,* and it is here that they are offered, morning and evening, as far as, by God's grace, the hand of every single man can devise.

Eph 4:11,12

Cf. Ps 132:9

Cf. Mt 21:13

Things of this kind, then, ought to be a wonder to the queen of Sheba, that is, to every holy soul who desires to look upon Solomon. They ought to be such a wonder that all the 'spirit' of worldly vanity should stripped away. To be truly 'queen of Saba' means to contemplate Solomon alone and be wrapt in wonder at the great and marvelous beauty of his holy church. When the incense of sacred zeal is found within a soul, and 'the land of incense' comes under her sway,* then she has become Sheba's queen.

Cf. 1 Kgs 10:10

6. But now let us listen to the praises of those other women who, with the queen of Sheba, contemplate the queen as she stands at the right hand of her spouse, 'in a garment of gold', surrounded with every kind of beauty.* 'Who is this', they say, 'who comes forth, rising like the dawn, fair as the moon, bright

Ps 45:9

as the sun, terrible as an army set in battle array?'*

Sg 6:9

If we consider the beginning and progress of the church, and take her very birth as the starting place for her story, then what meets us first of all is the loftiness of the angelic creation. The angels are certainly part of the church, untainted and sinless, set up as its pinnacle to bind it together and protect it.* Yes, and the angels are held in everlasting honor by God and by his whole church, because they have turned themselves wholly to the splendor of eternal brightness, escaping with all their strength from the dark shadows of perpetual night. The angelic host did not 'walk in the counsel of the wicked',* it was not corrupted by what was said to it, it was not stained by its free consent,* it was not contaminated by example. No, among the fall of so many thousands, amidst such violent temptations, it preserved immaculate the robe of its innocence.*

**Cf. Bernard, SC 27.6; SBOp 1:186; CF 7:79.*

Ps 1:1

Cf. Gen 3:6

Cf. Rev 12:4

So, from then on, the new creation, the future bride of Jesus Christ, throwing aside the shadows of the night,* became in all truth, 'rising like the dawn',* bringing forth from itself in labor the light, not only of holiness, but of eternal glory. That early-morning light shines brightly, about to create for the bride the day of eternity, and yet, it is not from itself that the light rises upon her, it is the sun, still unseen, that irradiates and prepares the dawn. It is described as 'rising', but indeed, it has already risen, because it has raised itself up to its creator with total unanimous consent. So one charity sets all on

Cf. 2 Cor 5:17

Sg 6:9

fire, and one wisdom fills all with light. That whole race of God's sons have all been formed in one conception, all brought to birth in one childbearing, all the same age with one birthday, all co-heirs of the one radiant joy.

7. But if, on the other hand, our desire is rather to see the dawn of this day as coming from our own mortal nature, Lucifer, who was indeed 'the son of the dawn,'* first darkened his own dawn, and then overshadowed ours, too. When we had brought darkness down over 'the face of the abyss',* in other words, his own face and that of his partisans, he immediately spread this darkness over our birth, defiling our first parents in their beginnings, and in them, staining all who would arise from them.* The dawn of the whole church on earth is clouded and overcast in consequence. But God showed the greatness of his mercies, and what had happened did not end in shame, but in glory. The shining rays of the true Light made our dawn able to drive away from itself the darkness in which it had arisen, and to conquer and free itself from the condition of its birth.

Cf. Is 14:12

Cf. Gen 1:2

Cf. Gen 3:20

What Lucifer did, then, only added to the weight of our glory. His dawning was immaculate, and it was solely by his free choice that he cast down himself and his followers. Then he defiled man's dawning and provided him with an unavoidable occasion for sin. But man, despite the ignobility of his first appearance, found his darkness irradiated by grace, and he struggles to rise, through humility, to where Lucifer arose in brightness. Man took vengeance for the injury done him by laying hold of the birthplace that belonged to the thief who had stolen his own birthplace. God is a just judge,* and he saw to it that Lucifer was paid back in his own coin and could never again recover what he had lost, while man recovered what had slipped from his hands and, at the same time, received what Lucifer had lost.

Cf. Ps 7:1

8. Therefore the church rises 'like the dawn', reborn by grace, driving out the darkness of her first birth by the light of her holy regeneration and the godly power revealed in her. It is a true rising, a rising to him who creates this dawn in her through his uncovenanted mercy. She rises to him, conforming herself to him with her whole heart, showing honor to him with utter reverence, co-operating with him with all her strength. In such, she rises so as to share, to some extent, in the birth of the Sun of Justice, transfering to her own rising the dawn of his blessed nativity, illuminating her rising from the wonderful splendor of his.

9. But, what, we may ask, is the reason why the rising of the dawn is followed by a reference to the moon, since it is during the night that the moon gives her light? Yet, for all that the church has escaped her original night, she still has a night, but a night full of brightness. Yes, even after the break of dawn, the church has night, she has a night while it is day. Of course, that night is 'as bright as the day',* especially when the moon shines in her full strength, but until the sun also shines, in his full strength, it is still night. Let me speak more plainly. While 'we see in a mirror and

Cf. Ps 138:12

dimly,'* while 'we walk by faith and not by sight,'* there is still darkness. The light of the moon is the brightness of faith; the light of the sun is the radiance of charity. These two great lights have been given us, to rule over the day and the night.*

1 Cor 13:7
2 Cor 5:7
Cf. Gen 1:16

Faith, through the light of knowledge, dissolves and tempers the darkness of our ignorance, while charity, through the radiance of wisdom, makes even light itself still brighter, and with its burning heat enkindles a flame that the light of faith alone has not the power to supply. Knowledge, in fact, which comes from faith alone, is cold, like the light of the moon, but all the same, it is a great light and illumines the blindness of man's heart. It shows the ways of life to those who go astray,* it reveals to man, in its light, even its own darkness, it shows a vision of heaven itself. The light of knowledge opens our eyes to God, creator of heaven and earth, it uncovers the mystery of the Word made flesh, it shows us, too, the holiness of faith, which is nothing else than to rely solely on the grace of our Redeemer.

Cf. Ps 16:2

It was a truly great light, this brightness that appeared to us 'who dwelt in the land of the shadow of death,'* when Christ glittered forth on us from the heavens. In him and with him, a light arose for us, delivering our night from its original darkness and taking out of their night those who had not yet obliterated their murk in the greatness of his light. For in this night, 'the Lord makes a distinction' between the sons of light and the sons of darkness.* Wherever the sons of

Is 9:2
Cf. Ex 9:4

night may be, even if they are in company with the sons of light, it is midnight; while on the other hand, for the sons of light, though living among the sons of darkness, God's light dwells with them. But of course, charity is even brighter, because of its greater heat, and the light of faith will turn to darkness if the light of charity does not reach it. Still, it is right and fitting that the light of faith comes first. It opens the eyes of the heart, it accustoms them to guide themselves by what they can see by night and it makes them ready for the stronger light to come.

10. Yet, just as this light is both the light of dawn and the light of the moon, so it has its stages. It has an early morning, it has a noonday, it has, too, an evening. Its early morn is the joyous rise of charity, its midday is the burning heat of charity, its evening is charity languishing with love. In the incarnation of the Son of God, it has a light like that of morning, in his cross the light of noon (for we read that Jesus was crucified at noonday), and in his death, an evening light, by which the Sun of Justice knows the time of
Cf. Ps 104:19 his setting.* Of course, he knows a setting which he has himself prepared from eternity, a setting he has chosen and accepted and for our sake, offered freely and lovingly to God the Father, to be 'a pleasing odor' before
Cf. Ex 29:31 him.* We can see why, in the wonderful light of God's very great love, the bride of Jesus, holy church, walks 'from brightness into
2 Cor 3:18 brightness',* no less than from charity into charity, singing to him with the melody of
Cf. Ps 92:3 the lyre,* 'Evening and morning and at noon,

I shall tell and proclaim.'* *Ps 55:17*

But how sad to think how often the clouds of indifference overshadow the church's 'day', how often the rain of sorrow and weariness hide it, how many storms of tribulation disfigure it, how swiftly the night of ignorance steals over it and cuts it short!

11. It is only when night has gone from its midst, and the moon, as scripture says, 'is no more',* that the full and noonday light of charity will reign supreme. Then it will not be 'evening and morning, one day,'* but only day pouring forth to day the Word of God,* only God's salvation being proclaimed from day to day.* What could it be but perennial and never-ending day, when those who live then will themselves 'shine like the sun'?* But surely, it will not be like that sun who rises even on wicked men and in whom the very animals have a share?* No, it will be like that great tranquil Sun, the only Son of his Father, who from the immensity of his glory, not only renewed the spirit of the church, making it like uniting it to the Spirit of his charity, but also renewed 'our lowly body, making it like the body of his glory.'*

Ps 72:7
Gen 1:5
Cf. Ps 19:2
Cf. Ps 96:2
Cf. Mt 13:43
Cf. Mt 5:45
Phil 3:21

It was for this that the church was chosen by him from all eternity, and to this choice is directed whatever God did or will do, until the church comes to the hour of its glorification. Everything served this purpose, everything 'in heaven and on earth, and in the sea and in the depth of the abyss.'* In short, it was for this that the virgin's Son was chosen, also, so that he might be taken up by the Word of God,* of whom the bride sings that he is chosen from

Ps 135:6

**Bernard, SC 78.8; SBOp 2:271; CF 40:135.*

Cf. Sg 5:10 among thousands.* He was chosen to give the bride the same ground for being chosen as her spouse has, namely, the everlasting charity of God.

12. Then, in the phrase that comes next,
Sg 6:9 'terrible as an army set in battle array,'* the spouse goes so far as to share with his bride his majestic throne of judgement. She is to sit
Ps 98:9 there with him, judging in justice* and 'rendering to every man according to his
Cf. Ps 62 works.* Then she will be 'terrible' in very truth, looking into the face of the eternal judge and reading out from it, as from some great scroll of God's laws, what his judgement is. With the angelic creation there to assist her, like 'an army set in battle array', there will be
Cf. Ps 149:6 a two-edged sword in her hands,* striking with relentless rigor. O, how terrible the church will look on that day, flaming with such zeal, overwhelmed with so great a responsibility, judging with such authority, speaking with such power!

Nevertheless, there is something very controlled about her, because we are told she is an 'army set in array'. For if even on that day,
Cf. Ps 77:9 God 'will not forget to be compassionate',* certainly neither will she. Judgement will arise from truth, but it will not come into being without mercy. Yes, God will judge his people, but he will take pity on his servants, and be compassionate with them, that is to say, the church. Therefore in order that everything be done aright, mercy will
Cf. Ps 85:10 meet with truth and play her part.* She will insist, anxiously and courageously, that her role is the more important because, as she

faithfully recalls, from that day on there will be no place or time for mercy.

And now, dearest brothers, while it is still within our power to do so, with thanksgiving* let us come before the God of mercy, seeing that 'he will make his face shine upon us and compassionate us.'* It was mercy that drew down to us from heaven the Father's only Son, who with that same Father and the Holy Spirit, lives and reigns, God, for ever and ever. Amen.

Cf. Ps 95:2

Ps 67:1

SERMON FIFTY-SEVEN

The beginning of the fifty-seventh sermon. How, in Adam, the church 'rose like the dawn', and then, in the light and brightness of the gospel, grew through the prophets into a double radiance, making it able to attack the enemies of the truth, 'terrible as an embattled army'. Also, thinking of the church of the heathen, how joyfully it flocked to faith in Christ; it was bright as the moon in the lives of its faithful servants, radiant as the sun in the teaching and charity of its pastors, terrible as an army set in battle array in the quantity and quality of its martyrs.

'WHO IS THIS who comes forth, rising like the dawn, fair as the moon, bright as the sun, terrible as
Sg 6:9 an army set in battle array?'*

The words of Wisdom have many levels of meaning. He is like a rich man's wine cellar, able to flow freely from one wine to another. He has, in fact, both light wine and strong, according to the resources of the buyers and the capacity of the drinkers. He has a wine he mixes for his friends, and another he offers to his best beloved. He has a wine he has trodden out for his household intimates, and another he has blended for a less robust generation. So, the words we have before us at the moment make very good sense if seen as referring to the times when the church longed expectantly for the coming of her spouse.

2. Indeed, from the very beginning of the human race, as if from the early dawn of its day, when woman came forth from the side of man,* Christ Jesus, spouse of the church, *Cf. Gen 2:22*
wanted to be seen in symbol in his workmanship. He wanted it to be a prophetic foreshadowing of himself, a promise, so that the hopeful expectancy of the just might be supported by this prophetic word from the yet unsullied lips of man. The fact that wrongdoing soon followed could not change God's truth or overcloud the fair skies of righteousness. On the contrary, it made it appear all the lovelier, so that 'where sin abounded, grace abounded even more.'* So Adam could *Rom 5:20*
say, with his son David, 'I have sinned, I have done what is evil in your sight, so that you may be justified in your words.'* Even Adam *Ps 51:4*
with his powers of understanding, still pure and unblemished must be considered to have understood the significance of this event, for he was the father of all the prophets, as yet unsinning, and prophesied in the power of the Holy Spirit;* and in him, as in the first *Cf. Lk 1:67*
faint touches of the dawn, the church began to quicken to her rising. In him, she brought to birth the Sun of justice, that from then on would glimmer out to her in faith and expectation.

From the time of Adam, then, or so runs the pious belief, there has been no wavering in the certitude of the church's faith and the

intensity of her expectation, right until the day when the Promised One appeared. Also, the light of dawn grew brighter moment by moment, and because God blessed Adam's posterity, the lamp of prophecy began to glow and to encourage man in his darkness, until the Sun was fully risen. Admittedly, neither the light of dawn nor the lamp of the prophets was strong enough to put the darkness to flight. That was reserved for the Light 'which illumines every man coming into this
Jn 1:9 world.'* Dawn does not shake off the night, no, not until 'the sun has risen over the
Gen 19:23 earth.'* All the same, its glory is far from unimportant. The charity of her spouse has come so swiftly to forestall her, that she arose on the world as it came into being, and from then on has never waned. She has known only an increase in her brightness. Yes, dawn marks the beginning of the day, but at the same time, it does not yet mark the end of the night.

3. This is why the advancing sunrise is followed by a reference to the brightness of the moon, to make it perfectly evident, as day stretches out to the light of dawn, that the shadows of night have been changed but not driven away. Night, therefore, the night of human blindness and misery, supports its faith, as if by the moon's light, with the lamp of prophecy. This was so very bright, and indeed is so to this very day, that the apostle Peter says of it: 'We have the prophetic word made more sure. You would do well to pay attention to it, as to a lamp burning in a
Pet 1:19 dark place.'*

Moreover, the Sun himself, in all his tranquil radiance, did not take from us the brightness of the moon. Quite the contrary, he chose to use it to give fuller testimony of his own light. In fact, again and again, he drew it to the attention of those among his disciples whose eyes were not very strong, and compared these prophecies with what he had done or what others had done to injure him. Sometimes, again, he spoke of them to make their faith more firm, and to help them to accept the scandal of his passion. It was, too, by this lantern that the Jews had their lack of faith confuted, when Jesus said to them, 'If you believed in Moses, you would also believe in me, for it was of me that he wrote.'* 'You search the scriptures, because you think that in them you have eternal life, and it is they that bear testimony to me.'*

Jn 5:46
Jn 5:39

4. Moreover, it is not only the Incarnation of Christ, or his death, that are irradiated by the light of this lamp. Almost every footstep of the Word made man, the very nature of his death, followed by the glory of his resurrection, all are lit up so clearly, as to make the passion of Christ itself a witness to his having come, and to make darkness a light for him, in its consolations.* Certainly, when the disciples were heartbroken after the passion, he used this lamp to bring them tender comfort; 'How then will the scriptures be fulfilled?', he said.* Just as Christ's passion is the world's redemption, so is it also the fulfillment of the scriptures and the brightest light of faith.

Cf. Ps 139:11
Mt 26:54

So, from the faith and hope of the expectant church, as from the dawn, there arose the

Sun of justice. First he showed himself to the world in deeds of glory and words of grace, and then he became hidden behind the cloud of the passion. Yet, in the end, his resurrection brought him glorious to a day of unshadowed brightness, all this taking nothing away from the power of this moon, but increasing it, consecrating it, setting it on a strong foundation. Here we have an instance of what the Word of truth himself told us, that 'there is one who sows, and another who
Jn 4:37 reaps.'* He wanted it to be clear that the word of gospel truth, which the prophet sowed, is reaped by the apostle and all who preach the truth.

5. There is every reason, then, to say of the church, 'fair as the moon, bright as the
Sg 6:9 sun',* because she is permeated with the light of the prophets and of the gospels. From now on she is irradiated by the loving combination of their mutual truth, and being made perfect, as far as is possible in this earthly day, she has the happiness of recognizing her beloved. All the same, as the apostle says, although sun and moon each light up the other with glory, still, 'there is one glory
1 Cor 15:41 of the sun, and another glory of the moon.'* Undoubtedly, it is in the light of the prophets that the bride walks forward to the truth of the gospel, but from the glory of the gospel she again moves forward, right on into the full vision of eternal light.

So the light of prophecy makes the bride 'fair', giving her a prophetic certainty on which to ground her hold of faith in the gospel, but the light of the gospel makes her 'bright', preparing her, through the mystery of the incarnation and passion, for the future glory of those chosen to share heaven's brightness. One light makes a promise, the other fulfills it; one makes a forecast, the other shows the reality. Where one rescues us from ignorance, the other illuminates us with the truth, and where one sheds a radiance, the other sets on fire. The bride receives beauty from the light of the prophets, but blessedness from the light of the gospels. So she becomes 'fair', when her faith in the truth brings her to holiness, and she becomes 'bright', when the Truth is revealed and wins for her the reward of eternal happiness.

From these two lights, the bride becomes so 'burning and shining',* that she can attack, unaided, all the enemies of the catholic truth. She threatens them with the two horns of light upon her forehead,* advancing in all the menace of her horned appearance, and they see her as not only invincible but 'terrible'. By this light, then, she refutes the Jews by revealing to them the face of Moses, by this light, she disperses, the darkness of the pagans. By this light, she confounds the wickedness of heretics, unmasks the pride of schismatics, reveals the deceit of hypocrites. Merely by this light, she is an accusation of the evil of false brothers, a reproach to the sloth of the tepid, a sure guide to those who walk in right paths. Just as light is a solace to healthy eyes, so is it unbearable when they are weak, and in the same way, the bride who is 'fair and bright' to her spouse, becomes 'terrible' to the enemies of the Light.*

Cf. Jn 5:35

Cf. Ex 34:29

Cf. Sg 6:9

6. Against the enemies we have just spoken of, she advances 'like an army set in battle array'.* She is armed with zeal for justice, she is girt with the sword of the Spirit, 'which is the word of God,'* she has God himself as the reason for combat and as her ally in battle and as her prize of victory. She fights for God and with God, and certainly in a way that pleases God, for she is not striving for vain glory or through envy of her neighbors, but only for salvation. What battle-line could be better arrayed than this, or rather, what could be more terrible than this? For here nothing is sought except truth and goodness, nothing is to be captured except the honor of God and the salvation of her brothers, the whole war has no other end than peace and charity.

Ibid.

Eph 6:17

The aforementioned words of the Song of Songs will have this interpretation, then, if they are taken as referring to the truth of the prophets and the gospels.

7. But if, on the other hand, these words are applied to the praise of the church which arose from the gentiles, then they will express the admiration of Zion's daughters for the gentiles' faith, as well as for their holiness, wisdom and patience. As a matter of fact, the way the dawn rises seems a very apt symbol of the speed, eagerness and greatness of gentile faith. It awoke from a sleep whose heaviness had been so long and so profound, and at the very first light of the Lord's birth, it sped towards him, like 'the rising dawn'. It broke free from the darkness of such a great want of faith to forestall, with eager devotion

the Sun of justice.

I say, 'forestall', because it did not wait for the Wisdom of God to come and discuss with it the sublimities he had seen and heard when he spoke at home with his Father.* It did not wait for the eight kinds of Beatitudes* through which he would mark out an eternal inheritance for his elect and hand it over to them.* Nor did it wait for when he would give his children, in simple words, the knowledge of perfect philosophy. But equally, this gentile faith did not await his dazzling display of miracles and virtues and his giving commands to sickness and health, to wind and sea, to every angelic and human spirit, even to the demons themselves. On the contrary, it would not allow even the time of his infancy to escape it, but in the lowly beginnings of that infancy, it sought out and recognized its creator.*

Cf. Jn 8:38

Cf. Mt 5:3-10

Cf. Ps 78:54

Cf. Heb 12:2

And so the faith of the gentile nations was swift in its speed, eager in its rejoicing, wise in its search, resolute in its finding, faithful in its adoration, generous in its gift of itself.

8. Is it not understandable that this woman (the faith of the gentiles), who was waiting in readiness for the hand of Jesus to begin its work, who even forestalled Jesus in his words, should deservedly arouse amazement and wonder in the daughters of Zion? The astonishing Wisdom of God himself found cause to marvel at and celebrate her, so that the daughters might well break out in her praise, 'Who is this who comes forth, rising like the dawn?'* Think of the faith of the centurion, at which scripture tells us that

Sg 6:9

Cf. Mt 8:10 Jesus marvelled.* In fact, he went so far as to
say that he had not found faith as great in
Cf. Mt 8:10 Israel.* That he was here commending the
faith of the gentiles is clear enough from what
he said to those who were following him. 'I
tell you most solemnly, that many will come
from the east and from the west, and sit down
with Abraham and Isaac and Jacob; but the
children of the kingdom will be cast out into
Mt 8:11 the exterior darkness.'* Then we have the
Canaanite woman who interceded for her
daughter, and when she was refused, persisted,
and by the great noise she made, battered at
Cf. Mt 15:22 the silence of Jesus.* When he turned away
from her, she followed him without apology;
she humbly adored him when he rejected her;
she listened patiently to his reproaches, and
so, in the end, she brought forth 'honey from
Deut 32:13 the rock, and oil from the flinty stone.'* I
repeat, in the person of this woman, the
church of the gentiles deserved to hear the
Lord Jesus say: 'O woman, great is your
Mt 15:28 faith!'*

Then there was the woman of Samaria,
who found the God of Jacob beside Jacob's
well, and in place of the water that does not
quench our thirst, drew for herself 'the fount
Cf. Jn 7:38 of living water',* so as never to know thirst
Cf. Jn 4:14 again.* She too is a figure of the faith of the
gentiles, and she was commended by the very
author of faith when he said to the disciples
who were asking him to eat, 'I have food to
Jn 4:32 eat that you know nothing about.'* He added,
'Lift up your eyes and see the fields, that
Jn 4:35 they are white for the harvest.'* Here he was
making unmistakable reference to the ripeness

and zealous eagerness of the gentile faith, which he considered food that he hungered after and would eat in the near future.

There is this same mysterious eagerness among the foreigners who were sent as delegates to beg to see the face of Jesus, though at this time the Jews were plotting about Christ's execution.* Their eagerness enabled the members of this delegation to hear: 'The hour has come, when the Son of man is to be glorified,'* and Jesus went on to explain the manner and greatness of this 'glorification': 'I tell you most solemnly, unless the grain of wheat falls into the ground and dies, it remains alone.'* In other words, he was saying that he was 'the grain of wheat', a grain that was to die, because of the Jewish lack of faith, but one that was to bear fruit in the faith of all the nations of the world. And there was the centurion, too, when Jesus was suffering and the faith of the disciples was exceedingly disturbed. He reached the full stature of a strong faith, and the crucified Jesus, whom others saw and fell away, scandalized, drew him forward in praise.*

Cf. Jn 12:20

Jn 12:23

Jn 12:24

Cf. Mt 27:54

9. What can I say that does justice to the dawn of the resurrection? The whole throng of the gentile people, full of faith, rose together in that dawning. The Jews turned away, but, through a great and unambiguous doorway, I do not say the gentiles admitted the Word of God or even that they brought him in, but they snatched him in with outstretched hands, laid hold of him and took him to their embrace. In short, from that very minute, the gentiles could no longer

endure to have their faith symbolized by images and mysteries. Like the dawn, they saw with joy that the Son of justice had arisen, because the radiance of a new grace was enlightening them. They saw it with joy, they received it with reverence, they peacefully gave it birth.

With that Sun, then, there rose also the gentiles, fully admitting the grace of his great goodness to them. They rejoiced with him in a brightness so freely given and so long a darkness being replaced by so great a light. Throughout 'the great congregation'* every heart and every mouth opened wide to give God very great and everlasting thanks. They praised the Sun, breaking in sudden splendor upon the first light of this dawn, for, as scripture tells us, 'the morning stars and all the sons of God rejoiced together',* and by this it means the holy companies of blessed spirits. Yes, they praised the Sun, but they also marveled at the serene rising of the early dawn, and it may well be that these 'sons of God' are no other than the daughters of Zion. The spouse describes them, after all, as being astonished by the 'coming forth' of this dawn, as being rapt in admiration and praise.

Cf. Ps 22:22

Job 38:7

10. The conversion of the gentiles, so unexpected and so spontaneous, from its very beginning gave the daughters of Zion and the spouse himself, great occasion to rejoice and celebrate. Now, if this is true of its beginnings, what of its day to day increase in the beauty of holiness? And of its radiance when the Sun is at its full? What of the invincible courage of its endurance? All this

contributes a crowning glory; it has perfected its weight of wonder.

The moon is lovely, of course, but it is subject to the sun and borrows its splendor from it, returning often to the sun, when its own light is nearly exhausted, to receive brightness from it. In this it is a symbol of the pure, humble life of those who are subject to authority. They receive the brightness that, like sunlight, irradiates their darkness, from the teaching and example of holy pastors. In the same way, to alleviate their darkness, more completely, they have been given stars to help them, namely, glorious works of piety and justice, springing from a heavenly motive and cleaving to heaven with sincere faith, selfless execution, zealous expectation. These stars know how to avoid the light of day and to hide themselves, modestly and prudently, from the gaze of men. They know how to shine for God alone, deep within the secrecy of their night, so that for all eternity, they can shine out for him.* And in fact, the moment these works are done for God and in the way he wants, they do not exist moment by moment, but they shine perpetually for God, endowed with a heavenly light.

Cf. Dan 12:3

As I have said before, this is the beauty of the moon: that the life of those under authority is humbly and obediently subject to those who, in the Lord, are placed over them. They endeavor to conform themselves to their superiors by obedience and charity, and whatever light they have, they do not even think of proudly comparing it with theirs. It is for those over them to shine like

the Sun, so that the moon may be able, as it ought, to borrow light from them. This too, is the beauty of the moon: that the brighter it becomes, the more truly it realizes its own darkness. It strives to equal the light of day so
Cf. Rom 13:13 as 'to walk honestly as in the day',* and it sets its face against the hidden deeds of infamy. It dispells night's shadows and gives
Cf. Rom 13:12 the lie to the works of darkness.*

11. But the sun-like brightness of pastors has for its purpose to shed a more lavish light. Indeed, in the words of scripture, 'You
Mt 5:14 are the light of the world.'* And again, our 'light should so shine before men, that they should give glory to our Father who is in
Mt 5:16 heaven.'* They ought to shine far and wide, those who are to be 'the light of the world', and to supply the very moon with brightness. Then the moon herself can give light to the world, not simply shine together with the sun. In fact, the light of the sun should be so very
Cf. Ps 72:7 great that moonlight, in comparison, 'fails'.* A light must be truly great to be enough for the whole world and to pour out over the moon, so that it too lights up the world, and all without diminishing itself in the slightest. This light carries its own fullness with it.

For the light of superiors, too, it is essential it should be so great that everybody fixes his attention on it. It should be of a nature
Cf. Jn 1:8 to 'bear testimony to the Light',* and so radiantly bright that it not only lights up the dark places, but the bright ones, too, and not only lights them up with what it teaches, but sets them on fire with what it does. With its sublime manner of living and lofty con-

templation, that sun approaches heaven, which is why it has the power to illumine everything with its light. So it ought to watch over everything with sleepless care, as Solomon says to the man who went surety for his friend. 'Go,' he says, 'hasten, importune your friend. Give your eyes no sleep and your eyelids no slumber.'* *Pr 6:3,4*

Consequently, if any cloud of adversity begins to lower, if any tempest of persecution beats down, if the thunder of threats reverberates and the gales of disparagement and insult bluster loudly, none of this ought to lord it over the sun, but rather to be its subject. We, of course, who walk on the earth alongside the animals, find these things evil and are quite rightly distressed by them, but God forbid they should affect the sun, shining aloft in the firmament. As far as we are concerned, the light of the sun is sometimes hidden and obscured, but if it is truly the sun, it knows no diminishment in itself. However, even if it was bestowed upon the world by God to give light, it still ought to turn aside fairly frequently, to have a time for peace and quiet.

12. In fact, after traveling the circuit of laborious care, the sun ought to know how to set and be at rest in the evening, when it enters the embrace of leisure. As Solomon points out, 'sweet is sleep to a laborer,'* and *Sir 5:11* night is made to follow day, so that the man who, throughout the day, has been 'a light to the world', may shine forth to God throughout the night and receive from him light both for the world and himself. In a word, just as

the world enjoys this sun all day for its enrichment, so for the sun, it is the night that gives it 'enlightenment in its delights.'* *Cf. Ps 139:11*

Let us give thanks to the eternal Light! He has poured himself out so lavishly upon the church of the gentiles. He has fashioned a dawn from the eager speed with which they believed in him; he has formed a moon from the pure way of life and humble obedience of its people and made a perfect sun from the glorious teaching and most fervent charity of its pastors. But as for those who have turned away from this light and gone back into the original darkness, or a darkness even deeper, they are no concern of mine. The sun that has turned into darkness and the moon that has turned into blood, have their own judge.* *Cf. Joel 2:31*

13. For the moment, let us concentrate upon what the spouse says in praise of his bride when he dilates upon her glory by describing her as 'terrible as an army set in battle array'.* *Sg 6:9* It seems to me that, when he says this, he is attesting the courage and generosity of the martyrs that came from gentile stock. Treating of these renowned warriors, I do not know which to admire first and foremost, their numerousness or their patience. For if you think of their number, it is like the stars in the sky, no number can be found, and the dauntless strength of their fidelity is also like the stars. Nothing makes them falter in their course and their light never fails, but only shines out more brightly in the night of the worst persecution.

Scripture says of their courage: 'Their sovereignty is exceedingly strengthened,'* *Ps 139:17* and of their countless multitude, 'If I count them they are more than the sand'.* Yes, they are the army of God, an army, as scriptures sees it, 'most powerful',* and for them, to be united in the cause of Christ means to have enrolled as soldiers to fight for eternal blessedness. For them, to confess Christ Jesus means to have put him under the obligation to confess them before his Father.* In their eyes, being 'bound because of Christ'* means to have received chains of gold, and they see the shame of nakedness as being clothed in a robe of happiness. They take the pain of hunger and thirst as being the most satisfying of spiritual feasts, and the confinement of a prison turns into expansion for the soul. For them, the gloom of darkness becomes a sparkling radiance, and the taunts of insults yield to the glory of being honored. However various the tortures that try them, they see them only as the voice of the Holy Spirit within them. They think that to have exposed their lives for Christ's sake means to have given them to Christ, and to have accepted death for Christ's sake means to have found life with Christ.*

Ps 139:18

Cf. 1 Mac 3:27

Cf. 1 Mac 3:27

Cf. Mt 10:52

Cf. 2 Tim 2:11

Yes, and it is truly 'an army set in battle array', because when it goes out to contend with the world, it does not advance into battle with the very least reliance on its own strength. It takes God as its helper,* puts him in command of the very vanguard of the army, and looks towards him unflinchingly, as to the captain of the combat, the ensign of steadfastness, the palm of victory. Indeed, it is through this arrangement that

Cf. Ps 52:7

Cf. Ps 119:91 'the day stands fast',* so that faith does not waver and so steadfastness be shattered. On the contrary, cleaving to the Lord God of hosts, the battle-line stands unconquered with the unconquered Christ. Yes, it proceeds in good 'array', for Christ goes first and the army follows. It draws its example from his pattern, it takes its confidence from his goodness. Its hope rests on his promise, its might on his assistance, its courage on his protection.

14. Obviously, he made a less orderly arrangement of the battle-line, the man who hastily snatched up a sword and overlooked his shield and even said, 'Even if I must die
Mt 26:35 with you, I will not deny you.'* This is why the maid servant who was portress rendered him defenseless and, to his lasting shame be it said, struck the sword from his hands, or, in other words, took away from him the ex-
Cf. Mt 26:70 pression of the devout confession of Christ.* This was only to be expected. For he did not advance in a well-ordered line of battle, he scorned to follow after, he strove to be in the vanguard, which was why he deserved to hear
Mk 28:35 one day: 'Get behind me, Satan!'*

But the lack of battle array in this soldier meant that, thereafter, the army of these who set out to war was well-ordered in 'battle array'. His example taught them not to put their trust in bow and sword but in the
Cf. Ps 44:6 Lord, their savior.* So, among the inhabitants of heaven, this army exults as a conqueror. They have him to give them glory whom they had as their champion in the battle and as the reason why they died. Now he is the reason why they reign in everlasting happiness, he

who is the church's spouse, our Lord,
Jesus Christ, who with the Father
and the Holy Spirit, lives and
reigns, God, forever
and ever.
Amen.

SERMON FIFTY-EIGHT

The beginning of the fifty-eighth sermon. That the soul that loves God makes an immediate beginning in perfection, and in such a way that it always thinks of itself as at the first stages. Likewise how, like the moon, it comes humbly up to the sun to seek grace, and then separates itself from the sun, confessing its unworthiness. But also how, like the sun, it is on fire because of love, and the way in which it shows itself terrible, because of the solemn dignity of its conduct.

'WHO IS THIS who comes forth, rising like the dawn, fair as the moon, bright as the sun, terrible as
Sg 6:9 an army set in battle array?'*

These words of praise have been devised with such careful artistry that for two days already, they have as it were occupied my lips and your listening ears. The wonder of the daughters of Zion holds us too, in an amazement as great as their own, and let us hope, by equaling their wonder, to have the privilege of being counted among their number. But what, by God's grace, has been said so far, has all been directed to the praise of the church. Your kind indulgence is now waiting to have the same words applied to some one soul that loves Jesus. To the best of my ability, I shall comply with your wishes, and you, too, must comply with mine, so that God will grant a happy outcome to the wishes of us both!

2. And first of all, I must confess that I would consider myself or anyone else unfit to wonder at and praise the Lord's bride, without our first having been given sight of her. Obviously the daughters of Zion were able to, and so could the queens and concubines, for they had actually seen her. Oh, that someone would grant me to catch sight, at least once, of such a soul, so that I might not see only her back, from behind,* but see her 'face to face'.* It is not her outward appearance that I would see, where perhaps she has 'no beauty of majesty',* no, but rather that within her that makes her spouse desire her, and where 'all the glory of the king's daughter lies.'* I would call my eyes blest if I could see,* because, or so I hope, my heart within me would grow warm and glowing with the very same fire of love the bride feels, and which makes her soul, whoever she may be, break into flame and melt within her. Yes, I, too, long to wonder, to join with the daughters of Zion, to break out into a cry of joy and praise, 'Who is this who comes forth, rising like the dawn, fair as the moon, bright as the sun?'*

Cf. Gen 33:23
Cf. Gen 32:30
Is 53:2
Ps 45:13
Cf. Mt 13:16
Sg 6:9

But, in fact, I am not wholly dull and sluggish, as, in these evil days, one may legitimately be. These are days when we see the church assailed on all sides, and not without reason, for her charity for her spouse has grown cold,* and this lukewarmness gives

Cf. Rev 3:15

Cf. Rev 3:16 rise to a sick loathing.* Yet, even today, a
Is 13:12 man can be found 'rarer than fine gold',* or to be more precise, the Lord has preserved for himself thousands of rare souls, to be a source of wonder, at least to the citizens of heaven. And what is marvelous, he himself, the only true marvel, marvels over them!

5. Well, then, let us use our faith to lay hold on one of these souls, at all events. Let us contemplate her and wonder at her and exclaim: Who is this, who can receive such praise from men and angels and God himself? Who is this whose holiness has so sudden and so luminous a beginning, so bright and so humble a progress, so splendid and ardent a perfection, so venerable and mellow a consummation?

Clearly enough, in the appearance of the rising dawn, the beginning of a dedicated way of life is typified very logically. It is usually a trustworthy indication of the whole life to come, just as the kind of sunrise we have is to our day. Take Paul as an example. Consider the dawn of his day, and see how, following on the serenity of that dawn, even the light of the moon increased and the light of noontime reached an intensity of heat in him, after which came the appropriate perfection of eveningtide. He himself, speaking of the sunrise of his own day, makes this comment: 'When he who had set me apart from my mother's womb . . . was pleased to reveal his Son in me, . . . I immediately found no
Gal 1:15 pleasure in flesh and blood.'* In fact, immediately stripping off 'flesh and blood', he put
Cf. Rom 13:14 on Christ Jesus,* and just as, in the night that

was past, there had been darkness in him, so now he was filled with the light of the rising dawn.

I have spoken too briefly, because the single night of this single soul grew to a brightness that illuminated the days of so many, and the serenity of this single dawn arose to give light to the whole world.

4. But why do I say, 'it arose', a term more in keeping my own tepid beginning, and that of those like me? No, that dawn did not merely 'arise', it 'rose up'! It rose up in all its strength, it rose up, the whole of it, totally, all together. It rose up, and again it rose up, as scripture has it: 'Rise up, rise up!'* It rose *Is 51:9* up, shaking off all fear and sloth, in the Spirit of freedom; it rose up, clothing itself in wisdom and humility, in the Spirit of charity. 'Rise up, rise up,' says the prophet, 'Zion, clothe yourself with your strength,'* *Is 52:1* in other words, the breastplate of justice, for the work of preaching the gospel. And, says the prophet, 'Clothe yourself with the robe of your glory,'* in other words, with wisdom *Is 52:1* and knowledge, to be a light of the world, to the glory of God.

What can I say worthy of those other souls, too, that resemble this one? In their zeal to be like perfect apostles, they have made contempt for all that the world has to offer the very beginning of a good life. They signal their entry on a life of christian service by setting violent hands upon the kingdom of heaven.* What great freedom and peace, *Cf. Mt 11:12* dearest brothers, are expressed in those words which today, on the birthday of our father *of Nursia, the 'father of western monasticism'.*

Benedict,* are figuratively applied in praise of himself and his blessed offspring! He seems to take it from the lips of the apostle and use it for himself and his sons, saying to Jesus, 'See, we have left everything and followed you.'* This is an enormous act of faith, my brothers, provided always that the rest of the day advances in keeping with its 'rising dawn'.†

Mt 19:27. Cf. Jerome, Commentariorum in Matheum *3.19.27; PL 26:138, CCh 76:172.*

Cf. Sg 6:9

5. But, tragic though it is, all too frequently the sparkling dawn is, after a little, obscured by clouds. Darkness and the shadow of death* overshadows the whole day, so that day turns to night and the night itself is under the sway of a gloomy turbulence.

Cf. Job 3:5

If this was indeed to be the outcome, why was this generation conceived at all'. And yet, those who fall away so shamefully from their race, who bring such disgrace upon it, prove themselves never to have sprung from that noble stock. Anyone who has gone away from our midst, not relying on the solid foundation of God, which has a sure and unwavering sign, has, in fact, never been in our midst.* True enough, these people have a dawn, but whatever its beginning may be, it will never go any further. Why is this? Surely because it has not 'risen up'. Rather, what it has done, tepidly and carelessly, is to 'arise', or else, still more tepidly and carelessly, it has not even arisen, but it has 'raised itself'. It has declined to that generation whose heart was not steadfast, whose spirit was not faithful to God.* So, although this generation may have seemed at the time to be 'rising', it has not risen up with the sons

Cf. 1 Jn 2:19

Cf. Ps 78:8

'who are born and rise up',* it has not risen *Cf. Ps 78:6*
up with God its salvation. And so, when these men bend all their strength to aiming their bow, we see them put to disgraceful flight on the day of battle,* running away from their *Cf. Ps 78:9*
enemies.

6. But every soul that is holy and reverent is wise enough to remember that it was the Sun that brought her into this morning brightness. She never lets herself forget those words of the apostle: 'You were once darkness, but now, light in the Lord.'* And this makes her *Eph 5:8*
thankful to rise up, at the rising of the light, to give thanks to the rising Sun, adoring God, as scripture says.* So she rises with the sun- *Cf. Lam 2:19*
rise and pours out her heart like water, firstly because so dense a night has covered the Sun, and this outpouring is one of grief and shame, like the blushing dawn. And then, she will bless God and take his praise upon her lips,* *Cf. Ps 109:30*
because he has called her into his wonderful light,* and this will be the serenity of the *Cf. 1 Pet 2:9*
dawn growing pale and silvery.

Any soul that Jesus brings into a state of such intense happiness, where he is ready to impart to it the actual experience of his love, and where Jesus blesses it from the very beginning of its conversion, looking at the soul and desiring its beauty,*such a soul is *Cf. Ps 45:10*
blessed indeed. But why should I have tried to intimate something in her honor, when the daughters of Zion will proclaim her as being, not 'blessed', but 'most blessed'.* *Cf. Pr 31:28*

7. Now, if the Sun of justice rises for those who fear God,* how much more for *Cf. Mal 4:2*
those who love him! For those who fear,

Ibid. 'healing' will rise in God's wings,* but for the lovers, something more radiant and blessed, God's love. The wings of the sun rescue the former from the foul darkness of sinners and bring them into the light of the just: for light
Cf. Ps 97:11 has risen upon the just.* The latter these wings carry up to the light of those who love and are loved.

The dawn of a soul that loves God rises up, I do not say, every day, but all day, never tiring. For if one truly loves, then each hour seems like the dawn of fresh love. It was of charity that it is written in scripture, 'I shall
Ez 36:26 put a new spirit within you,'* and, 'A new
Jn 13:34 commandment I give you.'* There is a sense in which what is perpetually new, is perpetually at the beginning. In fact, newness continually holds within itself its own beginning, so as to seem always at the point of starting, since it is wholly unaffected by decay or age.

So the bride deserves her praise, not really because she has made progress or because she once rose like the dawn, but because, like one who has this day begun to love, or rather, now for the first time begun to love, she says:
Ps 77:11 'Now I have begun.'* And what she has begun will progress like the dawn rising. Oh, if only a dawn would come every day to my listless and sleepy soul, at least now and then throughout the nights! Then, even though I may be asleep, I could say with holy Job, 'When shall I
Job 7:4 rise up?'*

Lk 1:42 8. But 'blessed among women'* is the one who never finds her sloth or idle slumber overtaking her. She makes a vow to her beloved, 'I will give no sleep to my eyes, to my eyelids will give no slumber.'* She rises up to her Sun, and will not endure being sundered from him; she perpetually irradiates herself in his light, and she renews herself by continually contemplating him. Yet, is it consistent with his praise of her that she should be hailed as 'fair as the moon'?* It is only in the night that the moon's beauty is remarkable. Can we say that the bride, too, has a night? She has indeed, but it is a very luminous night. It is so luminous that it is during the night that she goes to seek the one 'her soul loves'.* Yet perhaps, it is because she sought him in the night-time that she speaks of having sought him, rather than of having found.*

Ps 132:4

Sg 6:9

Cf. Sg 3:1

Ibid.

The bride, then, possessed considerable light by which to rise up and go about the streets and squares of Jerusalem.* True, but she did not possess full light, since the one she sought did not fall in with her. So, for a real bride, when her beloved is away, her one sole activity is to call him back to her and, as it were, to call upon the morning of the true Sun and to long for his rising. But until that actually happens, she must alleviate her darkness by pondering over her own personal failure, using it to provide her with a sort of lunar brightness. Of course, the more light there is in her pondering, the more clearly does her darkness manifest itself.

Cf. Sg 3:2

9. But she also ponders over the light, being neither unaware of her borrowing it from the Sun, nor ungrateful. She has learnt to ascribe both kinds of light to him and to rely on him for the light by which she knows both him and herself. Whether in self-reproach

or in praise, she says the same: 'Since you light my lamp, Lord, lighten my darkness, my
Ps 18:28 God.'* So to this Sun, also, the moon frequently returns, to draw light from it for her own use, and the more she shows herself to the Sun, the less she seems in her own eyes. Yet the very circumstance that diminishes her is precisely what makes her able to receive enrichment from him. That Sun, always wholly full of his own light, never needs the light of others and never wastes his own, but 'he resists the proud and gives grace to the
Jas 4:6 humble.'*

But once she has caught fire, the moon hastens to move away from the Sun, because when she looks within herself, she feels the shame of her weaknesses and thinks she is unworthy of being near him. This is why that true lover of Jesus said to him: 'Depart from
Lk 5:8 me, O Lord, for I am a sinful man!'* Likewise that soul whose faith aroused Jesus admiration: 'Lord, I am not worthy that you
Mt 8:8 should enter my roof.'* Yet, in a wonderful fashion, the more she withdraws from the Sun, the more the moon's crescents are bathed in light, because, as the True Sun has laid down as an axiom, 'everyone who hum-
Lk 14:11 bles himself, will be exalted.'* So the moon's approach to the Sun is both a confession of her darkness and an invocation of God's light. But her retreat is an admission of her own personal unworthiness and an expression of her wonder at God's eternal majesty.

10. The bride of Jesus says, then, with Simon Peter, 'Depart from me, O Lord, for I am a sinful woman.* And I am a most

unhappy woman, wholly unworthy to look upon your face, unworthy, too, to have you look on me. For, 'what have you to do with me',* Son of the living God, seeing that you are the all-tranquil Sun, the changeless Light, while I am but the ever-changing moon? I cannot even see my own darkness except in light borrowed from you. What interchange can there be between your light and my darkness?* Would it not be wiser for me to turn humbly away from you than to force myself upon you, shamelessly? For who am I, what is my father's standing, that I should dream of being able to be wedded to you, you who are the Father's only Son, having no equal among the sons of men or even the sons of God? So, I say, I shall go away. I shall flee from your presence, since what I am is out of keeping with your beauty and majesty.* Perhaps my flight will please you; perhaps you will look kindly upon your servant's humility.*

Cf. Jn 2:4

Cf. 2 Cor 6:14

Cf. Ps 139:7

Cf. Lk 1:48

11. Quite certainly, my brothers, it is these thoughts, or others like them, that engross the mind of the soul that yearns after divine love. When she anxiously reckons up her darkness, she longs, right enough, for the mystical marriage, but she can feel no confidence in herself, because of her unworthiness. Love draws her one way, and shame draws her back again the other. There the kindness of her most tender spouse encourages her to be bold, and here the sheer weight of her weakness checks her most forcefully. But Jesus himself steps into this debate to settle it. He rewards the humility of his handmaid by this decision: that he will fill her with the light

of the moon in her unprejudiced pondering over herself, while at the same time, he will bestow the sun's splendor in her pure contemplation of God. From the one light, which makes her beautiful, she becomes displeasing to herself, while from the other, in the very beauty that is now hers, she becomes God's chosen one because of her eagerness to be pleasing to him.

But just as the radiance of the sun is incomparably greater than that of the moon, so too is the force of its heat. In fact, the moon is quite without any of the heat with which the sun is so limitlessly inflamed. Furthermore, when the soul knows itself—this is 'the light of the moon'—it absorbs more shame and fear than love. But when it contemplates the goodness and majesty of God, then it moves forward into wonder and affection. So, from the humility of self-knowledge, the soul becomes beautiful and lovable, but it is the purity of its deep gaze upon God that bears it rapidly away to the kisses and embraces of its beloved. In the first, the soul's desire is to be made pleasing to God, but in the second, beauty is the object and love is intensified. There she shines with a light that, in comparison with the stars, is very bright, while here, looking straight at the Sun, she is transformed into the same likeness, and she herself becomes a sun.*

Cf. 2 Cor 3:18

12. But the light of this sun, just like the dawn and the light of the moon, has its stages. In short, it has a morning, and it has a noon, and it has an evening. It has its morning in contemplating God's uncovenanted goodness;

it has its noon in gazing at God's ardent charity; it has its evening in pondering God's infinite liberality.

Without any doubt, there is a real comparison between the first light of morning and God's uncovenanted goodness, which freely anticipated any action of our own. In no other way does grace so indisputably make itself manifest as in these completely uncovenanted interventions. Here we truly have 'the finger of God',* and a change wrought *Ex 8:19*
by the right hand of the Most High alone.* *Cf. Ps 77:10*
This is something that no sorcerer's philosophy or heretic's perversity can gainsay, the change wrought when light springs living out of darkness, when the dead are summoned from the tomb, in other words, when the wicked are justified in the very midst of their wickedness.

Also, I might well describe the fervor of divine charity as being 'noon'. It is at that hour the sun blazes in the full force of its heat; it was at the sixth hour that the Sun was crucified.* Certainly, no one has a greater love,† or **Cf. Jn 19:14* *†Cf. Jn 15:13*
rather, no thinking spirit is able to express or even form a mental concept of the light and fervor of this love, which made God not only willing to die for sinners, but even be crucified.

Lastly, 'evening' seems to belong by right to God's liberality, because it was at evening that the Lord rewarded the workers in the vineyard, taking his own liberality as his standard, not their deserts.* Clearly, as the *Cf. Mt 20:14*
apostle says, 'the wages of sin is death',* but *Rom 6:23*
it does not thereby follow that the wages of

virtue is eternal life! Rather, as he goes on
Rom 6:23 to explain, 'The grace of God is eternal life.'*
Those whom, in his pure liberality, God has
called, predestined, and justified, he even-
Cf. Rom 8:30 tually, in pure liberality, glorifies,* so that
'the mercy of God is upon those who fear
Ps 104:17 him, from eternity to eternity.'* Moreover,
for the soul that loves God, this evening
means infinite repose, since, knowing the
Cf. Ps 104:19 time of its setting,* it realizes who it is that
Cf. 2 Tim 1:12 she trusts.* More exactly, the soul knows
Cf. Sg 3:1 whom she loves.* She is quite certain that, if
the walls of her wretchedness and weakness
are broken down, walls where, during this
mortal life, the spouse stands without, look-
Cf. Sg 2:9 ing through the lattices,* he himself will
joyfully appear to her, face to face.

13. Yet, on the other hand, what does it
mean when she is described by the spouse
as being 'terrible as an army set in battle
Sg 6:9 array'?* Perhaps having praised the inner
beauty of her heart, the spouse wished
through the mouth of the daughters of Zion
to commend also the dignity she showed in
the stern expression of her face, and deport-
ment, the carefulness of her speech and the
honesty of her works, in the hope that by
learning to admire the qualities they might
also learn to imitate them. Surely it is of a
terrible appearance that it is said: 'The young
men saw me and withdrew . . . and princes laid
Job 29:8,9 their hands on their mouths.'* And a little
later: 'If I smiled at them, it was too good to
be true, and the light of my countenance did
Job 29:24 not fall to the earth.'* Yes, that is a 'terrible'
light, and in a way like a flash of lightning,

which does not flow from foolish mirth, which is not excited by careless 'levity, which is unbecoming.'* It is grace and love that irradiate that light, as if from a peaceful cloud. Certainly, it is not a light that 'falls to the earth', because it makes no vain attempts to ingratiate itself with others, only to be their light, through the grace of its charity. *Eph 5:4*

So, to perfect her beauty, the Lord's bride strives to bring herself to the highest standard of dignity, which, to the undisciplined and youthful maidens, seems very terrible, and for no other reason except that she is 'in array'. They regard her as an angel of God, or as the pattern and model of all the virtues, and some of them love her, and others fear her, but all of them feel an equal reverence. But put yourselves this question: what is it in her that they fear or reverence, since, like them, she is 'dust and ashes'?* Are they not contemplating in her, with open eyes, the majesty of the Lord of hosts? So she is 'terrible' to them, who have not yet come to the stage, perhaps, when they can find her lovable. But if she is truly a bride, genuinely a mother, she will do all she can to convince them of her lovableness, by her usual liberality, yes, by her accustomed charity and the eagerness of her prayers and services, to the praise and glory of her spouse, only Son of the Father, who with the Father and the Holy Spirit, lives and reigns, God, for ever and ever. Amen. *Cf. Gen 18:27*

SERMON FIFTY-NINE

The beginning of the fifty-ninth sermon. That when the spouse speaks of the 'orchard of nuts' and the 'fruits of the valley', the flowering 'vines' and the 'pomegranates', he is praising the same qualities in the bride as the daughters of Zion praised a little while before, but more soberly and discreetly.

'I WENT DOWN to the orchard of nuts, to look at the fruits of the valley, to see whether the vines had budded, whether
Sg 6:10 the pomegranates were in bloom.'*

It is not very clear whether this verse is to be assigned to the bridegroom or to the bride. The verse before it belongs both to the spouse and to the daughters of Zion, giving wonderful expression to the admiration both feel for the bride, and the verse that comes after seems to apply less to the spouse than to the bride or to the synagogue. Certainly, whoever it applies to, it is not the spouse, seeing that it runs: 'I did not know, my soul disturbed me, on
Sg 6:11 account of the chariots of Aminadab.'*

However, to get to work, let us first see, with your permission, in what sense these words are applicable to the spouse. In the praises we have just been discussing, the very last phrase of all is that the bride is 'terrible
Cf. Sg 6:9 as an army set in battle array',* which seems

to point unmistakably to the constancy of the martyrs. It is therefore in order to refer this and every other part of his praise to its proper quarter that the spouse commends his work and displays its fruits. For the daughters of Zion and for the bride herself, this is of the utmost necessity. Praise must be deliberately directed to have Christ as its object, although he, who alone deserves to be praised, generously shares with his bride what is said in his honor. He forms her praises on the mouths of those who praise him, and he who stirs them on to praise, is himself the rewarder and the reward.

2. Let us imagine the spouse, then, saying to the daughters of Zion, who are lost in admiration of the bride: 'You do well to admire and honor your mother, but first and foremost you must look to the reason for it all. It was my coming down from heaven that poured out all this light, dawnlight and moonlight and sunlight. It was my human weakness that brought about all this endurance, that gave so terrible an appearance to an army of martyrs. For I went down to the 'orchard of nuts,' coming forth like a bud from the shoot of Jesse's stump,* so that I might pass on to my native stock the lovely and sinless dawning of my birth.' *Cf. Is 11:1*

There is something very beautiful and fitting in Christ's describing the stainless purity of his mother, the blessed virgin, as 'an orchard of nuts', because it was from her that all this precious family of herbs arose. In fact, she came forth as the one sole shoot from the stump of Jesse,* and she gave birth to one Ibid.

sole flower. But see what has happened! From this shoot, thousands of shoots have grown, as many as the stars of heaven, and this one virgin is the mother of many, many virgins. She has brought them into the world through her pure chastity, just as she brought forth her Bud, on whom there rested the Spirit of
Cf. Is 11:2 the Lord.*

How could virgins long so eagerly for this way of life, if it had not been for the blessed Virgin who found this incomparable 'treasure
Cf. Mt 13:44 hidden in a field'?* Before her, absolutely no
Job 28:13 one 'knew the price of it',* and so there were few who valued it, fewer still who sought for it, fewest of all who found it. In general, virginity had less of praise than of insult and curse. Yet it was very fitting that the angel should bring to this virgin the good news that
Cf. Lk 1:30 'she had found grace with God.'* In other words, she found what lay hid, concealed from mortal eyes, in so far as the finding of it was reserved for her alone. She found the beauty of this grace, its fruit, its fertility, its glory. There was beauty in the dignity of its holiness, fruit in its restoration of our nature, fertility in giving rise to so many virgins, glory in its being mother to the Word.

You can see, without any doubt, how fruitfully the spouse 'went down' into this 'orchard'. But this 'going down' was not first
Jn 1:14 at the time when 'the Word was made flesh'* so as to dwell among us. He went down also at the time when, to sanctify the Virgin in the womb and consecrate her dawning and establish her formally in the state of holy virginity, he sanctified her, soul and body.

3. So the Blessed Virgin is the only virgin who is also a mother. Yes, it is she who is 'the orchard of nuts', because it is she who gives virgins birth, who is the model, the guardian and the glory of the chaste. She gives them birth, since she is the first and pre-eminent woman to pursue this state of life, and she has brought into the world the whole family of those who pursue this same grace. She is their model because, as if she were 'a shoot from the stump of Jesse',* her own 'Jesse', who is Jesus, she stiffens them to the full stiffness of what they have undertaken to live, and with her example, she forms them to the right shape. She is their guardian, enclosing them round like 'a garden enclosed'.* She defends them from the assaults of the foe and overshadows them to protect them from the violent heat of their own passions, just as the Holy Spirit overshadowed her.* She is their glory, because, in the regeneration of the saints, she will be the pride of those whom, for God, she brought to birth, formed and preserved in this grace of virginity.

Is 11:1

Cf. Sg 4:12

Cf. Lk 1:35

4. But you may say: What has been said is true enough, but how relevant is it? What connection do these words have with what went before? I answer: a very great connection, but one must concentrate. In this last verse, the spouse is recapitulating the praise of the daughters of Zion, when they extolled the bride with the most profound compliments and compared her holy beginnings to the stages of the rising dawn. Her humility, which looks only at the grace of God, as at the sun's brightness, they compare to the

light of the moon. Her charity they speak of as the sun, and her courage and steadfastness as an army set in battle array. The spouse graciously takes up these praises of Zion's daughters, pouring forth from the spring of the most disinterested charity, as much for their profit as for the sake of his bride. All the same, the form and the manner of these praises of theirs, he himself lays down.

5. He lays down the form, since he is himself the source of all their good qualities, and he is the reason why, amid all these admiring exclamations of theirs, they may well seem, in the light of their very great excess of admiration, to have rather under-expressed it. The manner, too, he lays down, as he clearly reduces their praises to a more modest measure. He refrains from any comparison with the luminaries of the heavens, and it is from things that can be shown as belonging to this earth of ours and that happen repeatedly here below, that he takes an image expressing a lowlier yet still noble form. So what the daughters of Zion intended to symbolize by the serenity of the rising dawn, the spouse has commended by referring to an orchard of nuts. In one place there is talk of the beauty of the moon, and in the other, the spouse touches upon the same quality but calls it 'the fruits of the valley'. What the daughters praise in 'bright as the sun', he praises in 'the budding vines'. What they describe as 'an army set in battle array', he seems to see as 'the blooming of the pomegranates'. On both sides, the same commendation is being given.

But the earlier form is more enthusiastic, as

befits young women. The spouse speaks with the greater sobriety, we would expect from him. And, of course, there is more wisdom in an admiration that takes its rise from God. His words are: 'I went down to the orchard of nuts.'* It is as if he were saying: My bride, the church, comes forth, rising like the dawn, because I have anticipated her, by my free gift, going down to the orchard of nuts, my mother. Since I was about to take flesh from her, I could consecrate her to myself. I could prepare her for the universal church, to become the salvation of her people, the mediatrix with God, the model of holiness, the patroness of virtue. *Sg 6:10*

6. Again, the church herself can be meant by 'the orchard of nuts', because the Lord has sent from Zion 'his powerful shoot',* the Lord Jesus, and that 'Zion' is the church is admitted unhesitatingly by all. So it is the church that is the orchard of nuts, a most pleasant and fertile orchard, teeming with trees that bud into the flowers on which the Spirit of the Lord finds repose.* Indeed, it is by the sanctifying power of the Holy Spirit that the flower of this holier way of life, at first a tender blossom that must change into the greater sweetness of the fruit, becomes eager to put to death 'all in it that is earthly'.* So it bears around in its body the cross of Christ,* almost as if it were some sort of protective shell that will guard and defend the sweetness of sanctity's dazzling whiteness. Yet it is not only the exterior affliction of the body that is sanctity's defense. There is also a far more bitter spiritual conflict, which sets *Cf. Ps 110:2* *Cf. Is 11:2* *Col 3:5* *Cf. 2 Cor 4:10*

itself to intervene between flesh and chastity and is never allowed to sleep, day or night. As if it stood in the line of battle, engaged in a perpetual struggle, by the very fierceness of its bitterness, it covers what lies concealed within, and keeps the sweetness safe.

But this orchard of nuts buds not only into shoots of righteousness, but also into shoots of amendment and reformation. In other words, there are not only souls keeping intact the glory of their chastity by a continual asceticism, but there those, too, who take pains to renew, by reforming their hearts and chastising their bodies, what is amiss, and to restore what is damaged. Of course, if a rod is cast heedlessly to the ground, it may sometimes be turned into a snake, by which I mean that the asceticism of a holy life, slipping out of our hand through sloth, may be led away, an entranced victim, by its own concupiscence. But even so, if we use the medicine of repentance, which is both the 'tail' of the
Cf. Ex 4:4 serpent* and the final end of chastity, and manfully take hold of the snake, the marvelous and merciful providence of God makes it return to righteousness and its former virtue.

Ordained priests, in particular, are obliged to both these forms of holy living, obviously so as both to fight for chastity themselves, and to lead and train others in this same warfare. This is undoubtedly why Aaron's rod is described as having blossomed more abundantly than all the rods of the other
Cf. Num 17:8 tribes, and to have borne nuts by a miracle.*
It was in memory of this that the shoot was

enshrined among the treasures of the ark of the Lord.* Yes, God's greatest treasure within the church is clerical celibacy, which gives rise to the rich fruit of salutary example for the whole church. If it ever loses its fertility, then the power of the clergy could still be a rod of fear, but it will not be a rod of guidance. It will be able to strike, to destroy, to shatter to pieces, but it will make nothing blossom and bear fruit in others, since it has not first shown in its own self the miraculous sign of its own blossom and fruit.

Cf. Num 17:10

7. So the spouse recalls how he went down into the orchard of nuts, since it was as a result of the first visitation of his grace that he planted what one could call a paradise for himself and his bride,* out of the young trees that made up the outstanding holiness of his blessed mother and the blossoming chastity of the other saints. Clearly, this paradise is indeed an orchard of pleasure, having nuts and fruits, having vines and pomegranates.* It was to inspect these things that, as he tells us, he went down to it. Moreover, his visit is not the passing and casual visit of a traveler, but that of a careful father of a family. A father is concerned with the progress of the household; what is well done, delights him, what is badly done, disturbs him, carelessness makes him annoyed, he is roused when there are things to be put right. The spouse has seen to it that he points out the carefulness of his interest. He explicitly says that first 'I went to look at the fruits of the valley', and next comes 'to see if the vines had budded.'* And he is not content just to 'see', he obviously

Cf. Bernard, SC 23:4; SBOp 2:140, CF 7:28.

Cf. Gen 2:8

Sg 6:10

came to try out dispositions, as well as to sanctify intentions, enkindle love, strengthen loyalty.

8. It seems to me that by 'fruits of the valley' he intends to signify the disposition of the humble of heart. This is delightful to taste and to scent, and a source of great pleasure to that heavenly gardener. There is a lovely taste, because these lowly ones have no knowledge of anything earthly or fleshly, but only of the devotion of a humbled spirit. There is a lovely scent, because they breathe forth the fragrance of angelic obedience, or, better, that of Christ, who, having gladly become for our sakes a free-will sacrifice, offered himself to
Cf. Eph 5:2 his Father as a fragrant offering.* And it was with trees that bore this fruit, that the Lord planted the paradise in which he placed the
Gen 2:8 first man he made.* Without a doubt, for the rational spirit, made in the image of its
Cf. Gen 1:26 creator,* just that minute called into being, the craftsmanship of everything around him forced upon his notice the majesty of his craftsman. Obviously this spirit learned to appreciate the majesty of his creator and the lowliness of his own position. The whole of
Cf. Col 1:16 creation both seen and unseen* gave a lesson in obedience either by its example, or by being ready at hand to sever him or at his side to help him.

So, being like this, paradise was a whole world of delights for man. Of itself, it brought humble thoughts to his mind, while from all sides it pressed upon him an awareness of God's grandeur. And to man, newly created and still innocent, there was something very pleasant about this food which he obviously did not possess 'in the sweat of his brow'.* *Cf. Gen 3:19* Rather, he possessed it in the brightness of his dawning* *Cf. Is 60:3* and in the light of the face of God,* *Cf. Ps 89:15* and it was like a banquet always and everywhere spread out before him. But what a tragedy! Because of the fruit he stole, unlawfully snatching at forbidden pleasure, these great joys became irksome to Adam and all his race.* *Cf. Gen 3:15* To this very day, the whole race of Adam has an ear open to the serpent, bringing lofty thoughts to his mind and dissuading him from humility.

9. But Christ, the new Adam,* *Cf. 1 Cor 15:22* the spouse of holy church, who came to retrieve the long-lost joys of man, was the only one of Adam's seed who did not lend an ear to the serpent's hiss or stretch out his hand to the forbidden tree. What he 'showed to the woman that God gave him,* *Cf. Gen 3:12* was rather the fruit of the valley, that is, the fruit of humility, and he told her, 'Learn of me, because I am meek and humble of heart, and you will find rest for your souls.'* *Mt 11:29* These fruits are fruits of salvation, fruits of life, fruits of happiness, and they spring from the fruit-bearing tree that is himself. It is from the stock of this tree that the other trees in this garden take their rise, so that they too can bring forth their fruit at their season.* *Cf. Ps 1:3* In the present time, the fruit that is found is great indeed, for it is rest for the souls of the humble,* *Cf. Mt 11:29* but in the time to come, it will be a still greater fruit, when 'everyone who humbles himself, will be exalted.'* *Lk 18:14*

So then the spouse went down into the

orchard of nuts so as to look at the fruits of the valley, because, once a holy way of living has borne fruit, he is glad to see humble thoughts in the heart. Otherwise, from its very holiness, the spirit may rise up with greater arrogance, and the virtue in which it is now taking foolish self-complacency, may begin to lose its appeal for the soul's judge.

10. After the fruits of the valley, the
spouse also looks for a rich yield from his
vines, and I take this to mean nothing else
than an abundant charity. This is surely 'the
Jdg 9:13 wine, that gladdens God and men,'* that
makes both God and men wholly intoxicated.
For can we not say that intoxication has
stolen up, apparently, on God himself, when,
having received a cup from the soul that loves
him, he falls into a heavy sleep, forgetting all
the wrongs done him in the past? Did not
omnipotence fall asleep on the cross, over-
Cf. Ps 78:65 come by this kind of 'wine'?* Was it not 'out
of the very great love with which he loved
Eph 2:4 us,'* that 'he poured out his soul in death'
and allowed himself to be numbered 'among
Is 53:12 the wicked'?* It is from the stock of this
vine that he comes to implant, in his orchard
of nuts, his chosen vineyard, commanding
charity and inspiring charity by telling his
Jn 15:9 beloved ones, 'Abide in my love.'* And he
urges them to brotherly love, also: 'A new
commandment I give you, that you love one
Jn 13:34 another, as I have loved you.'*

It is these two kinds of charity, namely, love of God and love of our brothers, that are the two vines he desires to see in bud, naturally expecting fruit to result from their flowers. The vine is in flower when our words reveal charity, when we have a holy longing to love God or our brother, when we pray devoutly to the Father of the spirits, imploring charity, when we listen devoutly to the Word whenever something about charity happens to come to our hearing. 'Flowers' like these give the spouse a firm pledge of charity, and so he comes to seek carefully for them, to observe them well, to look into them with solicitude. Consequently, it is part of his work to give shape to whatever in his vines he finds shapeless, to prune the sterile, to cut back the excess, to make flowers grow from the shoots and fruit from the flowers.

11. After the budding vines, then, the next thing is to inspect the pomegranates, the symbol, as we have already said, of the royal virtue of patience. This is fittingly joined to charity, which must of necessity be exercised in exercises of patience. Charity is only true when at last it has become patient.* Of course, human nature being what it is, it is impossible that patience should be found among us without the hammer of tribulation having worked upon it. But equally, charity that has not been tested by patience will be of little value, and patience which has not been shaped by charity will be altogether shapeless and of no value at all.

Cf. 1 Cor 13:4

So the spouse looks to see if the pomegranates have truly blossomed, that is, if holy souls are breathing out patience, meditating on it and longing for it from the very depths of their heart. He looks to see if it breathes out, not from their own virtue,

Cf. Jn 15:5 which is nothing,* but from him who is the *Cf. Rom 15:5* God of patience and all comfort,* since they wait for him with all the eagerness of sighs and groans and tears. It is, in fact, the crime of idolatry to hope for any virtue except from the Lord God of virtues, from whom and in *Cf. 1 Cor 8:6* whom and through whom are all things.*

To him be 'honor and glory
1 Tim 17 for ever and ever.'*
Amen.

SERMON SIXTY

The beginning of the sixtieth sermon. How these words may be applied to the church which, considering the weakness of her state in her various orders of men, admits that she 'does not know', something she can say of herself after being deeply disturbed by the chariots of Aminadab, that is, the terrible assault of judgements.

'I WENT DOWN to the orchard of nuts, to look at the fruits of the valley, to see whether the vines had budded, whether the pomegranates were in flower. I knew nothing, my soul disturbed me, on account of the chariots of Aminadab.'* *Sg 6:10,11*

In the previous sermon, I said that I could not make up my mind as to which of the two, spouse or bride, should claim these words of praise as their own, because what precedes them belongs clearly to the spouse, but what follows them to the bride. But all the same, this indecision, like almost every ambiguity of this kind in holy scripture, actively advances holy discernment. For indecision knocks on very many gates to find truth, and while it is held in uncertainty as to which will best give entrance to her, it finds entrance through every one of them. So a single uncertainty becomes the occasion of great richness of understanding; while it hesitates over which meaning is the better, the mind delves into all those possibilities and embraces one and the same truth in each of them.

I have discussed, by the Lord's gracious gift how these verses of the Song befit the spouse. Now, with your encouragement, let us see how God's grace makes them also applicable to the bride.

2. We find the bride, then, stirred by the glorious praises of her spouse and the daughters of Zion, and 'disturbed' by these words,
Cf. Lk 1:29 as we read of the Blessed Virgin.* She stands there, taken aback, hesitant as to what meaning she should give to so ardent and thoughtful a commendation. This is why she 'goes down', then; she wants to 'see' and 'look at' each separate thing that is extolled in her honor. As far as can be inferred from her words, she is not uplifted by what has been said in her praise, so much as cast down by what she ponders within herself. In fact, the words that come from her lips to ring in the ears of the spouse, are those of a soul that has been cast down and made lowly. 'I knew nothing,' she says. 'My soul disturbed me on
Sg 6:11 account of the chariots of Aminadab.'*

3. So, if the verse before this one also belongs to the bride, she seems to have found the occasion for this 'disturbance' in what she claims to have 'seen' and 'looked at', when she went down to the orchard of nuts. Certainly, this is something completely different from what the daughters of Zion contemplated in her, or thought that they con-

templated, and which made them proclaim her 'blest among women'.* She herself, looking very carefully in her orchard, finds there matter to arouse grief rather than approbation. This is not surprising. There is no doubt that if any earnest seeker after truth were to enter today into the orchard of nuts, namely, into the life of those who have taken a vow of chastity by accepting priestly ordination, and should diligently consider them, would not such a man, if he has any religious feeling within him, be very soon embarrassed by his entry into the 'orchard'? Would he not be disturbed and say, with a groan; What has become of all that the daughters of Zion found to celebrate?

Cf. Sg 6:8

Certainly, in that enormous plant that, swollen with honor and riches, has spread far and wide throughout the land belonging to the master of the household, you will find very few shoots of the noble stock from Jesse's root.* You will find a mere scattering of flowers upon whom rests the Spirit of Jesus.* Nearly every shoot that you behold will have been turned, by a terrible and awesome portent, into a serpent.* If you are wise, your preference will be to flee from the sight of them and to avoid their bite, unless it should happen that, at God's command, supported by spiritual strength and faith, you take firmly in hand the task of loving correction. This would mean putting a restraint on wanton behavior, straightening out what has become crooked, healing what is poisoned, reforming all that is deformed. All the same, wherever you turn your eyes, you see that, today,

Cf. Is 11:1
Cf. Is 11:2
Cf. Ex 7:12

God's church is in the hands of men such as these. They bear over the people a rod of authority,* (*Cf. Mic 7:14*) the power to control everything, at least in so far as it pertains to their own hand and dignity and to the protection of that honor.

4. Yet, when you look closely at this rod, you find there no trace of the blossoms of Aaron's rod,* (*Cf. Num 17:8*) by which I mean the high priest, Christ. You find there no trace, or very little, of the fruit that shoot bore. Churchmen of today possess Aaron's rod, right enough. They possess it in the lessons of the gospel, in the creeds of their faith, in proclaiming their fidelity to it, in the sacred symbol of baptism, in the sacrament of the altar. They possess it almost as if it were stored within the ark, that is, within their consciences. But it is as a witness against them, not as a wonder and an inspiration. They do not apply themselves to taking from that shoot patterns of virtue, so that they themselves may blossom and bear fruit for God. No, their concern is rather to make use of that shoot to give them the appearance of spiritual freedom, so that they may blossom into high office and bear the fruits of luxurious living. But the time will come when this shoot of the nut-tree will become for them a rod made of iron.* (*Cf. Ps 2:9*) Or surely since it is having now already turned for them into a serpent, it will bite them with a most deadly bite, which no age ever to come will see healed.* (*Cf. Deut 32:24*)

6. When there is such barrenness and disfigurement in the orchard of nuts, what yield of fruit can be expected from the valley

of the multitude under authority? 'I looked on the earth,' says Jeremiah, 'and see, it was waste and void; and to the heavens, and they had no light.'* What wonder if, looking at the life of people under authority, everything there seems empty and as if reduced to nothing,* when all the light of teaching and goodness has disappeared from those who extend above them, like the heavens. According to the prediction of another prophet, we will see those 'heavens' melted away like smoke, filled with nothing but the vanity of worldly pomp, smoking with the worthlessness of earthly vapor.* Is it any wonder, therefore, when the very heavens have vanished away, that the earth, too, should revert to its original chaos, so as to become, as in the beginning, 'waste and void'?*

Jer 4:23

Cf. Job 17:7

Cf. Is 51:6

Cf. Gen 1:2

Without a doubt, this is what we are seeing happen today, this is what we lament at seeing: throughout the Lord's orchard, a very great scarcity of fruit, except what has been taken as a cutting from the forbidden tree and planted there.* It is, in fact, to what has been prohibited, that the hands of Adam's sons stretch out in rivalry, struggling against God's commands, pressing forward to what he forbids, turning away from the wholesome, eagerly pursuing the destructive. Once they had fallen, through their eating of the forbidden fruit, it was of course, more wholesome to renounce deceptive pleasures and, following the remedy of repentance given them, to eat their bread in the sweat of their brow.* There would have been hope, then, that some day God might pardon the repen-

Cf. Gen 3:3

Cf. Gen 3:19

tant, and lead the exiles back to their own country.

To this very day, however, their hands are stretched out to the tree of falsehood. All the day long, they are taught by their great unhappiness how bitter is the taste of this tree, and what is meant by 'the knowledge of good and evil'.* Yet their greed to seize hold of this kind of fruit never ceases. So when the bride goes down into the orchard of nuts, it is this kind of 'fruits of the valley' that meet her on every side, and it is with these apples that she feels herself 'crowded round'.* To put it plainly, their scent is a torment, and the sight of them induces faintness.

Cf. Gen 3:22

Cf. Sg 2:5

6. But she goes on, to see whether 'the vines have budded', in other words, turning her attention to the way of life of those who have left everything* and seem to have undertaken the path of evangelical perfection. These men have vowed themselves solely to the charity of Christ, as if they were the vines of the Lord of Hosts that he expects to bring forth grapes at the proper season.* But even here, the bride finds her expectations flatly disappointed.

Cf. Lk 5:11

Cf. Is 5:2

How tragic that in very many places the flowers and fruits of these vines are cut short by one danger or another! They are either stripped away by the excessive cold of an enormous sluggishness, or torn to pieces by the fierce hailstones of discontent, or they rot in the foul vapors of fleshly appetites and empty ostentation. The shame of it is that, here on earth, their only glory in the sight of their fellowmen is their apparel. They put all their strength into a rich show of vine leaves and tendrils, pretending that beneath them is a rich supply of fruit. But wickedness, in its pretense, deceives itself, and it also deceives men who only see outward appearances.* The spouse, though, is not mocked.* He notes the differences between flowers and foliage, he can tell grapes from their wild counterparts. And the bride, too, can distinguish between them, especially since she is not content merely to see. No, she looks at them carefully, for she has certainly been taught by her spouse to know them by 'their fruits',* not by their foliage.

Cf. Ps 27:12

Cf. Gal 6:7

Cf. Mt 7:16

7. After investigating the vines, she turns her eyes to the pomegranates, prepared to see whether they are in flower. I think that what is symbolized here are those who have received the care of these same vines. My reason is that under the one rule of religion and the carefulness of one solicitude, as if under one skin, they have to defend and safeguard the one heart and one mind* of many, as if it were one body of many grains. It is the burden of this ministry that, round about the very beginning of her song, the bride sighs at having had it laid upon her, because it seems to be rather strongly opposed to the joys she is finding in love. Her words are: 'They made me keeper of the vineyards, but my own vine I have not kept.'* All the same, though, she patiently takes the burden on her shoulder for the sake of her beloved's will, and she receives as her reward a double gift of praise from him. For she hears: 'Like a broken pomegranate, so are your cheeks, concealing

Cf. Acts 4:32

Sg 1:5

Sg 4:3 what lies within.'* And then, secondly, she hears: 'Like a rind of pomegranate, so are
Sg 6:6 your cheeks, concealing your secrets.'*

The bride's 'cheeks', of course, are modesty and patience, and they are there to shelter and protect the grains of faith entrusted to her from the trials that beset her on every side and to which she must of necessity almost constantly expose her 'cheeks', as if to the burning furies of the sun or torrential rains. This is obviously a most difficult charge and a very heavy burden, for while she is forced to busy herself with external matters, that summon her out to look after temporalities, she all the time desires much more to be occupied with those that call her to return within, directed heavenwards. This is a torture that, as it were, held her up, spread out on a cross. She has but one consolation, that the anxious work of one means repose for the many, and she willingly offers her cheeks to receive distress, so that, like a sort of pomegranate skin, they may more safely foster a great number of grains.

8. The bride goes, therefore, to see if any apples are flowering in her garden from these seeds, and as far as she is able to observe from those which, being exposed to view, allow of open inspection, she is disturbed by the results. Without a doubt, this class is today almost non-existent. A very large number of us are ready of our own accord to offer our hands to those who take us captive, acting as if we were going away as guests, not at all as
Cf. Ez 1:14 if we were 'a flash of lightning',* we go away,

and we do not come back again. It is shaming to admit how our belly has cleaved to the earth,* and we have turned from angelic happiness to take on the form of things that creep. We have left all that is heavenly, we concentrate on the inheritance of the old testament, and we range ourselves with 'Israel according to the flesh'* to talk of the earth, to savor of the earth, to follow after all that is earthly.* If, as the Truth tells us, what fills the heart can be gauged from what comes forth from the mouth,* then, when we all come together in community,* it is these earthly matters that are heard in our conversations. It is the things of earth that we sow with a generous hand, and reap with plenty.*

Cf. Ps 44:25; 1 Cor 10:18; Cf. Jn 3:51; Cf. Mt 12:34; Cf. 1 Cor 11:20; Cf. Mt 6:26

It is failures like these that make the bride grieve over the misfortunes of her spouse, or rather, grieve with him and feel deeply disturbed over her own failings and those of her people. When she hears the enormous compliments the daughters of Zion pay her, she looks well at her condition. Instead of encouraging her admirers, she turns rather to herself to exclaim: 'I knew nothing, my soul disturbed me, on account of the chariots of Aminadab.'*

Sg 6:11

9. When she says, 'I knew nothing', it has two meanings. She is either telling us that she blames herself, and shrinks from what she sees, or she is saying that she wavers, uncertainly and with hesitation, as to what kind of judgement she should come to. For this is a time when even the church of God's chosen, completely enveloped in a cloud of obscurity, still dwells in darkness. Here on earth, the

Cf. Mt 13:29 grains of wheat are hidden beneath the chaff,* and while this is so, it would be rash to pass sentence on the conscience of another. The man who appears today as among the chaff, God, who judges from within, will one day number among the wheat. So, whatever the bride believes she has seen and looked at, she is very wise to leave the assessment of it to him who sees the heart. For herself, she says,
Sg 6:11 'I knew nothing',* in this one phrase protecting the reserve of her modesty, as well as curbing the judgements of the maidens, who for slight reasons jump to conclusions, either praising or deriding.

10. The bride adds: 'My soul disturbed me, on account of the chariots of Amina-
Ibid. dab,'* I would take 'the chariots of Aminadab' to signify the divine judgements of unfettered Truth, which is Christ Jesus. My reason is that it is somewhere said in scripture of these judgements: 'Their wheels were burn-
Dan 7:9 ing fire.'* And again: 'Their wheels are like
Is 5:28 the whirlwind.'* And yet again: 'Your thun-
Ps 77:18 der crashed in the wheels.'* Then there is Ezekiel, too, where we have four wheels, each having 'a wheel within a wheel', and every
Cf. Ez 1:15,16 wheel, in consequence, faces four ways.* And in Zechariah there are four chariots, each
Cf. Zech 6:1,8 of them drawn by horses of a different kind.* But since it would be very long and wearisome to explain each of these separately, let this suffice for the time being: that the wheels of fire represent the amazing speed, the very great acuteness, the unfathomable severity of God's judgements.

11. God's judgements are spoken of as

chariots because it is as if they move on four wheels, justice, prudence, fortitude and temperance. Justice is eager for the glory of divine honor, for we know that the honor of God delights in right judgement.* Prudence, exactly opposite, balances justice, so that zeal for distinguishing between motives and evaluating the intention has knowledge to control its fervor, to keep one wheel from exceeding the other, or being exceeded by it, by a hair's breath. Fortitude looks to the everlasting changelessness of God's judgements, something which is clearly a very marked feature of the verdicts God gives. And here the necessary balance is provided by temperance, and God compassionately tempers the severity of his sentence in the vessels of mercy that are called for. *Cf. Ps 99:4*

Moreover, the bride is correct in assigning these chariots to Aminadab, since 'the Father has given all judgement to the Son,'* whom the bride here has called 'Aminadab'. It is as if she wanted to give the reason why he has every right to sit one day in judgement, since it was his free decision to stand before his Father to be judged, for the sake of the people he had chosen.* When she speaks of 'the chariots of Aminadab', the bride is suggesting, too, that the strictness of the judge-to-come is closely related to the meekness of the one-who-was-judged. *Jn 5:22* *Cf. 1 Kgs 3:8*

12. But when she says, 'on account of the chariots of Aminadab', she can be taken as referring to whichever alternative you prefer: either to her previous words, 'I knew nothing', or to what she says next, 'my soul disturbed

Sg 6:11 me.'* It makes good sense if she says that she 'knew nothing' with respect to what sentence should be passed on what she has seen of the different states of the church, preferring to leave this to the judgement of her 'Aminadab', His 'judgements are true, righ-
Ps 19:9 teous in themselves,'* that is, having a justice that takes its base and certitude from the pattern set by eternal Truth. But, on the other hand, certainly, 'My soul disturbed me, on
Sg 6:11 account of the chariots of Aminadab,'* that is, the secret judgements of God, which seize with such speed and rightness upon those who seem to be standing on the topmost peak of virtue, and hurl them down to the depth of viciousness, because of their arrogance and ingratitude. And then, with equal speed and justice, they raise to angelic splendor those who were lying wretchedly in the dust, hideous with foul corruption, and they raise
Cf. Ps 113:6 them because they are humble.*

13. So the bride declares: 'My soul disturbed me, on account of the chariots of
Sg 6:11 Aminadab,'* so that I am not moved in the least by all these praises of the daughters of Zion, whether they are queens or concubines, no, and not even by the praises of my spouse himself, not even if he were to compare me to an angelic loftiness. I know the flying swiftness of those chariots, for scripture tells me that they were rightly described as 'whirl-
Cf. Ez 10:13 ing wheels' by the Son of man himself.* Yes, they are whirled through the air, now from the heights to the depths, and now up again, from the depths to the heights. This is why the sound of the wheels brings to me the

unmistakable and frightening sound of the judge,* and when I hear, I shrink away from their onslaught. *Cf. Ps 77:18*

Moreover, I fear, I tremble in panic, because of my own private 'orchard of nuts'. I dread that, when the Lord goes down into it, he will find fault with it for being barren. And I fear, too, that he will repudiate my 'fruits of the valley', as rotten or bitter or unripe. My 'vines' also: I tremble to think that, when he looks at them, he may say: I expected you should bring forth grapes, and you have brought forth wild grapes.* And then, I am in suspense as to what he will think of my 'pomegranates', in case it happens that my spiritual men themselves, though they may have begun 'in the Spirit',* will now end with the flesh. *Cf. Is 5:2* *Cf. Gal 3:3*

14. But in this terror I have a great comfort, that it is Aminadab who is master of these chariots, and his very name speaks of meekness and tenderness. It is for this precise reason that judgement has been given by the Father to the Son of man,* so that men are to be solemnly brought before a Man for their judgement. From that human countenance they are to expect humanity and mercy, to the honor, glory and splendor of the same only Son of the Father, who with his Father and the Holy Spirit, lives and reigns, God, for ever and ever. Amen. *Cf. Jn 5:22*

SERMON SIXTY-ONE

The beginning of the sixty-first sermon. How the praises we have been speaking of cause the bride anxiety rather than pleasure, and warn her to ponder carefully on herself and on God's mysterious judgements.

'I WENT DOWN TO THE ORCHARD OF NUTS, to look at the fruits of the valley, to see whether the vines had budded, whether the pomegranates were in bloom. I knew nothing, my soul disturbed me, on account of
Sg 6:10,11,12 the chariots of Aminadab.'*

I could, at this stage, move on and decide to make no more comment on all those points to which by its insistent search for the word of God, this marriage song rightly demands attention. But to do this would be to deprive the bride of her rightful praise and you of the fruit you deserve. I shall be glad insofar as I can to accede to her demands whatever they may be, but there is another obligation, to work for your growth in virtue, since it was for that you chose me as your abbot.

2. But there is one thing I want to warn you of in advance, as you may gather from the last part of this sermon, and that is the way the bride seems to have laid aside her former serenity of life, as well as taking to herself a sorrowful lamentation, in place of a

song of love. For it is from a throat hoarse with grief that the sad and plaintive sound is uttered: 'I knew nothing, my soul disturbed me, on account of the chariots of Amminadab.'* The reason for this sorrow and disturbance, as far as it is allowable to venture on an opinion about the Lord's bride, seems to have been derived from what has gone before. She says: 'I went down to the orchard of nuts, to look at the fruits of the valley, to see whether the vines had budded, whether the pomegranates were in flower.'*

Sg 6:11

Sg 6:10

In fact, what she hears are the daughters of Zion and the queens and the concubines, packed closely together like a huge army come to overwhelm her with their admiration. They seem to her like a terrible conspiracy, from which she very humbly and wisely retreats within herself, feeling exceedingly fearful. In what concerns herself, she dare not take the risk of believing any man's judgement in preference to her own. In fact, even when it comes to her spouse himself, who she knows quite certainly cannot be deceived, she is not lulled into security by his praises. She does not allow herself to snatch her peace from them, for though she knows he is her spouse, she does not forget that he is also her judge. The spouse, for his part, approves so warmly of his bride's charity, that he looks ardently, too, on 'the humility of his handmaid'.*

Cf. Lk 1:48

Finally, the bride recalls how she once heard of the sublime title that was given by the heavenly spouse to a certain noble lady, and how the name she was given made her

swell with pride, and immediately she fell and perished. She had this said to her: 'A green olive tree, fair with goodly fruit: this is what
Jr 11:16 the Lord once called you.'* And this was followed by the very terrible sentence: 'but with the roar of a great tempest, a great fire rose up in it, and its branches were con-
Ibid. sumed.'* These words of God are very high praise indeed, in fact, overwhelming praise, but they weigh down so heavily that they crush, they glow with such heat that they burst into flame, they rise aloft only to plunge into the depth.

3. So there is good reason for this holy and gentle soul to suspect that she has heard, in the measureless approval of the daughters of Zion, not only a cry of approbation, but rather a peal of thunder, or else a trumpet blast. Hence, apparently, her reference to 'chariots'. Certainly, a frightful swirl of sound bursts upon the ear when chariots rush forward, as it says in scripture: 'The sound of
Ps 77:18 your thunder in the wheel.'* Yet, by saying 'chariots', which contain several wheels, the bride seems to have intended a symbol more dread than that of the psalmist, who heard 'the sound of thunder' in a single wheel.

So, as if the daughters of Zion and the throng of queens and concubines were facing her like an army ready for battle, the bride draws up her battle array to oppose them. She treats their praises as if nothing but artful snares, and regards their admiration as concealed espionage.

4. At any rate, she goes down to her orchard of nuts, certainly examining every

corner of it with vigilant scrutiny. She sifts and weighs everything that is in it, nuts, fruit, the flowers on the vineyard, the pomegranate shoots; looking to see if the flowers have bloomed all the same, or the pomegranates budded. Moreover, before inspecting anything else in the nut orchard, which is where she goes first, it is my opinion that she makes a scrutiny of her personal chastity. She knows very well how passionately her beloved values this virtue, for it was his choice to flower in and from the shoot of a nut tree, that fairest and straightest shoot that grew from Jesse's root.* The bride, too, is eager for this flower, in order that the flower of a chaste heart, the Lord Jesus, may blossom in her and from her, but she is always conscious, in her very contented and humble examination, that she has been wedded to him in a manner completely different from that of the Virgin, so uniquely and pre-eminently chaste, who was taken up at the incarnation of God's Word, by a most special privilege.

Cf. Is 11:1

Then she lifts her eyes to all that blossoms and is fruitful in this garden, and I am referring to the glorious modesty of the saints. Some of them were sanctified in their mother's womb, guarding with the most delicate watchfulness the privilege that has been bestowed on them. Others were washed all over, when they rose up from the waters of baptism,* and by the grace of the same Spirit that brought them back to life, they have kept intact the purity of that holy washing, given to them from heaven. The bride looks carefully and thoroughly at her spouse's orchard,

Cf. Sg 6:6

and as she looks, she marvels at the sweetness of the flowers like this that grow there, and at the fertility of the nuts and the towering gracefulness and straightness of the shoots.

Prominent are those who have risen superior to the custom of the marriage bond, through the force of a stronger intention. They have declared war on their own passions, striving to overcome the very fact of their being human. To pursue this with greater ease, they have girded themselves with weapons that are powerful in God's cause, and well suited to this kind of warfare: scarceness of food and drink; poor clothing; perseverance in watching, working and praying, and all the other exercises of a dedicated life, with which they labor to bring about in themselves the refinement of a winning gracefulness of behavior.

5. This gracefulness of his bride is so pleasing to the heavenly bridegroom, that he delights to hear her praises being sung. He is pleased to hear it said of her: 'Who is this coming up, like a column of smoke, per-
Sg 3:6 fumed with spices?'* Clearly, just as slenderness makes a woman's beauty more pleasing, so fatness diminishes it. Moreover such is straightness or uprightness of the shoots, that there is nothing in these holy souls, whether in their walk or appearance, their speech or their actions, that is either suggestive or deceptive, nor is there duplicity in their motives. No, they have nothing in common
Cf. Mt 25:1 with 'the foolish virgins',* their only desire is to give pleasure to the one they seek to
Cf. Ps 45:6 marry, and to be like rods of righteousness,*

rods of God's kingly power, rods in the hand of their God.* *Cf. Is 62:3*

6. It is these things that the bride ponders over in the great orchard of her spouse. She examines into them very carefully, and immediately afterwards runs back to her own little bit of garden, and sees, with shame and sorrow, what she is lacking. On the other hand, though she grieves at seeing her own defects, it only makes her rejoice in the progress of others. Since she is the Lord's bride, and charity knows nothing of envy,* *Cf. 1 Co 13:4* she understands how to find compensation for her own loss, in the profit others make. All the same, she is careful, during this inspection, to keep hold of just so much distress and humiliation as she thinks necessary to arm her conscience against the daughters of Zion, who are ministers to her own presumption, should they suddenly assail her ears.

No, even she, bride of the Lord though she is, even she—I say this quite confidently—has something in her orchard that causes her to feel shame rather than self-satisfaction. She is no better than her fathers,* *Cf. 1 K 19:4* who humbly admitted to having been given 'a sting of the flesh', an angel of Satan to harass them without respite, so that they might not take pride in the greatness of their spiritual favors.* *2 Co 12:7*

7. As for the bride, if she is the daughter of her fathers, or rather, since she cannot be their unworthy descendant, since this is simply not possible for one who has been privileged to be wedded to the spouse of heaven, she must certainly groan in the

Cf. Ps 38:8 bitterness of her heart.* At the times when she feels herself troubled by shameful desires, *Cf. Rm 7:23* as if she was in captivity to the law of sin,* like a maid servant sitting enslaved at the *Cf. Is 42:13* mill,* she will certainly groan and cry out **Cf. Rm 8:23 †Rm 7:24* and exclaim,* 'Unhappy creature that I am,† what possible connection can there be between *Cf. Is 11:1* me and the heavenly flower of Jesse's stem?* O, if only the daughters of Zion could see who they were comparing to the dawn, the *Cf. Sg 6:10* moon, and the sun!* O, if only they would go down, here and now, into this orchard of mine where grow my nuts, and look deeply at the twisted, shapeless and sterile things in it, they would surely turn their eyes away! They would surely change their tune!

O daughters of Jerusalem, when I consider the fruits of the valley, by which I mean the delicious produce of humility, borne by so many different trees in the orchard of my spouse, and then turn to the produce of my own fruits, what heart do you think is left to me? I measure myself against those who have given posterity an everlasting memorial of their obedience and humility and respect for God, who have left to their heirs the clear imprint of their virtues. Humble in the sublimity of their virtues, sublime in the excellence of their humility: compared with these, my humility deserves no praise at all.

I find my greatest delight in being 'encom-*Sg 2:5* passed by these fruits',* smelling so sweetly of all perfumes, especially when my beloved is not with me, and I find myself in a *Cf. Sg 2:5* languishing state.* I realize then that I need the comfort of such perfumes to make my languor bearable. Indeed, much of my good health is due to them, seeing it is the sweet scent of the obedience and humility of my lord and spouse that I draw into my nostrils.* They are incentives, spurring me on to love, making me vividly aware, through their perfume, their taste, their beauty, of the presence of my beloved.*

Cf. Eph 5:2

Cf. Bernard, Gra 14.51; SBOp 3:203; CF 19:111.

8. These are the fruits of a true and holy 'valley', the humility of the Most High God. It is truly a valley, a valley pleasant and fertile, a green valley, brimming with light. It is not just a vale, but a real valley, enclosed on all sides by the hills, clearly a place made for friendly companionship, for harmony, for sympathy. This is what the bride seems to be implying, when she speaks of a 'valley' rather than a 'vale', so that, coming down from the dark mountain of his majesty, that majesty should himself become the valley to this vale of ours, by suffering our pains and sympathizing with us, by giving us all that is his, and accepting in return, all that is ours. So, if there is any humility, obedience or submission that does not have the taste of that heavenly humility, that is, does not derive its form and motive from that source, as from its own true root, then the bride can only regard it as fruit growing wild.*

Cf. Rm 11:17

9. After examining her fruit, the bride turns her eyes to looking at her vines, anxious to discover whether they have yet budded.* Here, of course, we have what seems to me a very appropriate symbol of the practice of two kinds of charity. The bride never rests, day and night, from lifting up her heart in

Cf. Sg 7:12

love to her spouse, at one time wondering at his eternal wisdom and holiness and all the other 'glory that is his, as the only Son of the
Jn 1:14 Father,'* and then again glorifying the goodness, patience and humility that made him stoop to being born of his virgin mother. The bride concentrates carefully on these two kinds of vine, both of noble stock, devoting herself wholly to this task, taking great pains to prevent anything being found in her vineyard that is sterile or less fruitful, because of neglect. If these vines go on to bud and then, by God's grace, the fruit reaches its customary ripeness, the bride is confident that she will rejoice her spouse's heart with their produce, and she hopes this will make him ready to grant her these wedding joys.

10. But here is a further question: what did the bride mean the vines to signify when she says that she wants to see whether they
Cf. Sg 7:12 have budded?* Has it not been true for a long time, that her beloved is all hers, and she is all
Cf. Sg 2:6 her beloved's?* Moreover, surely the spouse has already drunk deep of this wine, and declared it excellent, so that she herself, delighting in his cheerfulness, declares that it is fit for her beloved to drink and to savor on
Cf. Sg 5:1 the lips and in the mouth.* But of course, when she says this, the bride's humility and fervor appear in all their magnificence, because she looks upon herself as a lover who has only just begun to love. What else could she mean to signify by 'the budding vines', except the tender, winsome beginnings of love? The time when these buds begin to show themselves is obviously when the words and works of the

Lord Jesus fill the meditating mind with sweetness, when the bride's mouth parts with longing to draw in the Breath of God,* when her heart swells with sighs of love. It is then that everything that bears on the charity of Christ is sought after eagerly, read about with relish, listened to joyfully, related with feelings of delight.

Cf. Ps 119:131

As far as I can see, when the bride directs her gaze to the vineyards that are planted on the mountains of heaven, of whose richness the blessed who live in God's house,* drink deep, day and night,* she comes to the conclusion that her own vines have not yet flowered. She turns her thoughts, too, towards the charity of her forefathers, which was as fruitful as it was generous, and enabled them to say, with a clear conscience, 'The charity of God has been poured into our hearts, through the Holy Spirit who has been given us.'* At that time, the love, 'which is in Christ Jesus',* overwhelmed sin, and to her it seems that her own love has as yet borne no fruit.

Cf. Ps 84:4
Cf. Ps 36:7
Rm 5:5
Cf. Eph 3:19

But how can she feel when she thinks over the very abundant and luxuriant fruit of her spouse himself? Surely the bride has every reason to call her vineyard sterile, when she compares it to the richness of the vineyards which Christ makes blossom, with eternal fruitfulness, in the land that he has promised us?* Even if she should see something growing on her vines, she will feel right to wonder whether it is really a flower, with its promise of fruit, or not something that counts as foliage rather than flower. It is clear that she

Cf. Mt 5:5

is beset by the same suspicion about the flowering of her pomegranates. Here we see her motherly solicitude, since, as I recall saying above, under one protective rind, she cherishes many children, as if they were many children, as if they were many seeds united within one body.

11. Yet she seems to doubt also, whether
this loving solicitude of hers is in every
respect pleasing to God, whether it is per-
Cf. 2 Co 6:6 fumed with true and unfeigned charity,*
such as Christ revealed and commanded and
Cf. Jn 13:1 lived out to the end.* To put it in another
way, she doubts whether her solicitude has
Cf. Sg 7:12 yet begun to blossom.* She hears a definite
form of brotherly love laid down for her in
Cf. Eph 5:2 the law of her God, and a definite amount.*
The form is, that as Christ loved her, so she
Cf. 1 Jn 3:14 must love her brothers.* The amount is, that
she should give up all that she has, most
Cf. 2 Co 12:15 freely,* and then give up her very self for
Cf. Rm 9:5 her brothers' salvation.* The form is, to
watch sleeplessly over the safety of the souls
whom Christ redeemed; the amount is, for
their sake, with Christ, to lay down one's
Cf. Jn 15:13 own soul.*

About both these things, the bride's sight seems to be clouded by uncertainty. She does not know whether she really possesses the true form of this charity, and she knows far less what she has achieved with regard to its measure. In what concerns herself, she has learnt not to trust too readily in her own feelings, and whatever she is persuaded of in her own regard, she does not put more weight on it than actual evidence warrants. It was a wise man who said: 'What does he know, who has not been tempted?'* So, for all these reasons, the Lord's bride has become for herself a great subject that she must query, and since she wholly despairs of her own ability to penetrate the great abyss of her own heart, she says: 'I knew nothing; my soul disturbed me, on account of the chariots of Aminadab.'* *Sir 34:9* *Sg 6:11*

12. As I said in the previous sermon, I think that the bride means 'the chariots of Amminadab' to stand for the whole of God's judgements. Roundness stands for his justice and their flying speed, for his wisdom, their power, for his dauntless strength and their balanced proportions, for his impartiality. It is on these four 'wheels' that the chariot of divine judgement rolls forward, and scripture usually sets them before us when it wants to inspire us with fear of this awesome judge. Indeed, as the prophet tells us, they are terrifying to behold, as well as to hear.* What David says is true: 'The sound of God thunders in the wheel.'* What normal person, pondering over the depths of God's judgements,* would not tremble at the sight of them? Who would not shake with fear at hearing them as from a peal of thunder, when in a moment, God takes pity and the sinner is instantly and freely saved from the depths of wickedness, and then, God judges, and a righteousness of great perfection and long duration vanishes in a flash? *Ez 1:18* *Ps 77:18* *Cf. Rm 11:33*

The bride, then, concentrates steadily and cautiously on the terrible sight of the wheels and their frightening sound. Never is there a

better time for this than when she sees herself entreated and incited by shouts of admiration from the daughters of Zion, and they present a public spectacle that laps around her like a blockading army. The more they praise her, the more she shrinks. They think they can see into her spiritual life, and it is on this precise point that she replies that 'she knows nothing'. The very things they bring forward to reassure her soul, she confesses that her own soul finds 'disturbing'. They exult the special graces given her, but she thinks always of the depth of God's judgements. In short, she sets herself to be ready in advance with an imperviousness to everything and everybody who praises and glorifies her, so that she may be all the more pleasing to her beloved, the less influenced she is by human renown. She offers her
Cf. Jm 4:12 spiritual life to be judged by him alone,* to whom the Father has justly given all judge-
Cf. Jn 5:22 ment,* who, with the Father and the Holy Spirit lives and reigns, God, for ever and ever. Amen.

CISTERCIAN PUBLICATIONS INC.

TITLES LISTING

THE CISTERCIAN FATHERS SERIES

THE WORKS OF BERNARD OF CLAIRVAUX

Treatises I: Apologia to Abbot William, On Precept and Dispensation .... CF 1
On the Song of Songs I–IV .. CF 4, 7, 31, 40
The Life and Death of Saint Malachy the Irishman .... CF 10
Treatises II: The Steps of Humility, On Loving God .... CF 13
Magnificat: Homilies in Praise of the Blessed Virgin Mary [with Amadeus of Lausanne] .... CF 18
Treatises III: On Grace and Free Choice, In Praise of the New Knighthood CF 19
Sermons on Conversion: A Sermon to Clerics, Lenten Sermons on Psalm 91 .... CF 25
Five Books on Consideration: Advice to A Pope .... CF 37

THE WORKS OF WILLIAM OF SAINT THIERRY

On Contemplating God, Prayer, and Meditations .... CF 3
Exposition on the Song of Songs ... CF 6
The Enigma of Faith .... CF 9
The Golden Epistle .... CF 12
The Mirror of Faith .... CF 15
Exposition on the Epistle to the Romans .... CF 27
The Nature and Dignity of Love .. CF 30

THE WORKS OF AELRED OF RIEVAULX

Treatises I: On Jesus at the Age of Twelve, Rule for a Recluse, The Pastoral Prayer .... CF 2
Spiritual Friendship .... CF 5
The Mirror of Charity .... CF 17†
Dialogue on the Soul .... CF 22

THE WORKS OF GILBERT OF HOYLAND

Sermons on the Song of Songs I–III .... CF 14, 20, 26
Treatises, Sermons, and Epistles .. CF 34

OTHER EARLY CISTERCIAN WRITERS

The Letters of Adam of Perseigne, I . CF 21
Alan of Lille: The Art of Preaching . CF 23
John of Ford. Sermons on the Final Verses of the Song of Songs, I–IV .... CF 29, 39, 43, 44
Idung of Prüfening. Cistercians and Cluniacs: The Case for Cîteaux .. CF 33
The Way of Love .... CF 16
Guerric of Igny. Liturgical Sermons I–II .... CF 8, 32
Three Treatises on Man: A Cistercian Anthropology .... CF 24
Isaac of Stella. Sermons on the Christian Year, I .... CF 11
Stephen of Lexington. Letters from Ireland .... CF 28

THE CISTERCIAN STUDIES SERIES

MONASTIC TEXTS

Evagrius Ponticus. Praktikos and Chapters on Prayer .... CS 4
The Rule of the Master .... CS 6
The Lives of the Desert Fathers ... CS 34
Dorotheos of Gaza. Discourses and Sayings .... CS 33
Pachomian Koinona I–III:
The Lives .... CS 45
The Chronicles and Rules ..... CS 46
The Instructions, Letters and Other Writings of St Pachomius and His Disciples .... CS 47

** Temporarily out of print* *† Forthcoming*

Symeon the New Theologian. Theological and Practical Treatises and Three Theological Discourses . . . CS 41

Guigo II the Carthusian. The Ladder of Monks and Twelve Meditations . CS48

The Monastic Rule of Iosif Volotsky . . . . CS 36

CHRISTIAN SPIRITUALITY

The Spirituality of Western Christendom . . . . CS 30

Russian Mystics (Sergius Bolshakoff) CS 26

In Quest of the Absolute: The Life and Works of Jules Monchanin (J. G. Weber) . . . . CS 51

The Name of Jesus (Irenée Hausherr) . . . . CS 44

Entirely for God: A Life of Cyprian Tansi (Elizabeth Isichei) . . . . CS 43

Abba: Guides to Wholeness and Holiness East and West . . . . CS 38

MONASTIC STUDIES

The Abbot in Monastic Tradition (Pierre Salmon) . . . . CS 14

Why Monks? (François Vandenbroucke) . . . . CS 17

Silence in the Rule of St Benedict (Ambrose Wathen) . . . . CS 22

One Yet Two: Monastic Tradition East and West . . . . CS 29

Community and Abbot in the Rule of St Benedict I (Adalbert de Vogüé) . CS 5/1

Consider Your Call: A Theology of the Monastic Life (Daniel Rees et al) . CS 20

Households of God (David Parry) . . CS 39

CISTERCIAN STUDIES

The Cistercian Spirit (M. Basil Pennington, ed.) . . . . . . CS 3

The Eleventh-Century Background of Cîteaux (Bede K. Lackner) . . . . . . CS 8

Contemplative Community . . . . CS 21

Cistercian Sign Language (Robert Barakat) . . . . CS 11

The Cistercians in Denmark (Brian P. McGuire) . . . . CS 35

Saint Bernard of Clairvaux: Essays Commemorating the Eighth Centenary of His Canonization . . CS 28

Bernard of Clairvaux: Studies Presented to Dom Jean Leclercq . . . . CS 23

Bernard of Clairvaux and the Cistercian Spirit (Jean Leclercq) . . . . CS 16

William of St Thierry: The Man and His Work (J. M. Déchanet) . . . . CS 10

Aelred of Rievaulx: A Study (Aelred Squire) . . . . CS 50

Christ the Way: The Christology of Guerric of Igny (John Morson) . . CS 25

The Golden Chain: The Theological Anthropology of Isaac of Stella (Bernard McGinn) . . . . CS 15

Studies in Cistercian Art and Architecture, I (Meredith Lillich, ed) . . CS 66

Studies in Medieval Cistercian History sub-series

Studies I . . . . CS 13

Studies II . . . . CS 24

Cistercian Ideals and Reality (Studies III) . . . . CS 60

Simplicity and Ordinariness (Studies IV) . . . . CS 61

The Chimera of His Age: Studies on St Bernard (Studies V) . . . . CS 63

Cistercians in the Late Middle Ages (Studies VI) . . . . CS 64

Noble Piety and Reformed Monasticism (Studies VII) . . . . CS 65

Benedictus: Studies in Honor of St Benedict of Nursia (Studies VIII) . CS 67

Heaven on Earth (Studies IX) . . . . CS 68†

THOMAS MERTON

The Climate of Monastic Prayer . . . . CS 1

Thomas Merton on St Bernard . . . . . CS 9

Thomas Merton's Shared Contemplation: A Protestant Perspective (Daniel J. Adams) . . . . CS 62

Solitude in the Writings of Thomas Merton (Richard Anthony Cashen) . . . . . CS 40

The Message of Thomas Merton (Brother Patrick Hart, ed.) . . . . . CS 42

FAIRACRES PRESS, OXFORD

The Wisdom of the Desert Fathers

The Letters of St Antony the Great

The Letters of Ammonas, Successor of St Antony

A Study of Wisdom. Three Tracts by the author of *The Cloud of Unknowing*

The Power of the Name. The Jesus Prayer in Orthodox Spirituality (Kallistos Ware)

Solitude and Communion

Contemporary Monasticism

A Pilgrim's Book of Prayers (Gilbert Shaw)

Theology and Spirituality (Andrew Louth)

* *Temporarily out of print* † *Forthcoming*